Ninety More
Pipe Blends:

90 more recipes with 90 color labels

by Robert C.A. Goff

Dreamsplice
Christiansburg, Virginia

Ninety More Pipe Blends: 90 more recipes with 90 color labels

Dreamsplice
3462 Dairy Road
Christiansburg, VA 24073

www.dreamsplice.com

ISBN: 978-1-7333979-7-1
Library of Congress Control Number: 2022904288

Contents

Other Books by the Author

Non-fiction by Robert C.A. Goff

**Grow Your Own Cigars: growing, curing and
finishing tobacco at home**
**Blend Your Own Pipe Tobacco: 52 recipes with 52
color labels**
How to Read a US Roadmap
Climbing Out: Grand Canyon Hikes 1997-2006
**Just Walking Home: Appalachian Trail Hikes
1996-2013**
**In the Ozone: collected essays, poems and non-
fiction**

Fantasy-fiction by Robert C.A. Goff

Ternaria: Legacy of a Careless Age

Science-Fiction by Robert C.A. Goff

**Impact Mitigation and other Science-Fiction
Short Stories**

Fantasy-fiction by Robert C.A. Goff and Micah M.A. Goff

The Counterspell Chronicle
Counterspell: Guardian of the Ruins
Counterspell: The Second Law
Counterspell: Age of Fools [upcoming]

Acknowledgments
(from Blend Your Own Pipe Tobacco. Dreamsplice, 2018)

As I write this, I am 70 years old. So the list of those individuals who have contributed to my enjoyment and understanding of pure tobacco pipe blends over the past half-century could easily fill these brief pages. I will leave out most, and expect that they will never notice the slight. I will, however, offer a salute to my late friend, Lance Meagher, who first introduced me to English and Balkan style pipe tobaccos so long ago. Also to those no longer on this earth, I owe a debt to Craig Tarler, of Cornell & Diehl, whose sage advice guided my earliest blending efforts.

Over the years, I have personally grown over 100 distinct varieties of tobacco—a scant sampling of the thousands that exist. Some of the more rare varieties were grown from seed graciously provided by Paul Wicklund, of NorthwoodSeeds.com. In addition, Don Carey, of WholeLeafTobacco.com has generously offered me many dozens of samples of unique, commercial tobaccos, straight from the bale or barrel, to evaluate and enjoy. And Anton Eise de Vries, of CdF Domitab, has shared personal samples and seed, first from Indonesia, and subsequently from the Dominican Republic. Likewise, members of the FairTradeTobacco.com forum have happily shared many other varieties of seed, finished leaf that they either grew themselves, or that came into their hands from other forum members from across the world, and even samples of their own personal blends. These latter folks are too numerous to list, so I hope they will forgive my omission.

With the assistance of a number of other brave souls, I developed over the last decade, techniques for home tobacco kilning and kiln construction, home tobacco flue-curing (initially using a steel trash can!), home fire-curing, making small-batch Perique and making Cavendish on a kitchen stove. My attempt at making Latakia at home was a failure, since Latakia's distinctive aroma depends on smoke from woods that are not available to me. While I feel that I accomplished a lot with that list, much of my insight derived from the efforts—both successful and unsuccessful—of others.

Pure tobacco pipe blends are a constantly evolving exploration. Even the famed Balkan Sobranie Smoking Mixture—White (approximated by my *Balkan White* blend), evolved over the years of its success and availability, including changes in its proportion of Latakia. The collection of 52 pure tobacco pipe blends that I offer here is a snapshot of a single point in time. Tobaccos change, specific harvests differ, and smokers' tastes drift over the years. While these blends are my own, they are the fruit of input from numerous people over many years, and are informed by my past delight over fabulous commercial pipe blends that are no longer available in their original formulation.

R.C.A.G. (2018)

For *Ninety More Pipe Blends*, Fair Trade Tobacco Forum member @GreenDragon (Steven Farmer) has graciously contributed a chapter on Specialty Yeast Perique. Traditional perique is made using the random and ubiquitous yeast, *Pichia anomala*. Steven has explored utilizing intentionally added yeast strains (such as those used for making red wine, or for brewing beer) for making perique. This results in yet another potential set of interesting blending components for your pipe tobacco.

R.C.A.G. (2022)

Introduction

Ninety More Pipe Blends is intended as a companion to my January 2019 book, *Blend Your Own Pipe Tobacco*. There is no duplication of material or blend recipes. During the intervening four years, I have cracked the nut on making Latakia at home, and explored a new, simple way to make cut plug (sliced flake). And of course, I spent much of the time making experimental pipe blends, and settling on new, tasty blending recipes.

Since I enjoy creating attractive labels for my blends, every blend in this volume provides one. Sometimes the label graphics are inspired by the blend, and sometimes an interesting graphic inspires the creation of a new blend. An example of the latter is **Red CAVEndish**, a blend inspired by a photo of a huge red cave. It is not always a coincidence that an image of my shredded blend closely resembles the graphic or animal shown in the label. Occasionally, a photo is the conceptual source of the recipe, such as the silhouette photo of the cows in the **Contrarian** label.

There have been a few instances when a new blend just pops out of my imagination in its final form. That is fairly rare. Instead, I make a trial blend, make adjustments, make another trial blend, and continue the cycle, until I'm satisfied that it captures what I intended. That latter method, labor and time intensive as it is, always serves to further clarify my understanding of the balances of burn and aroma and taste and acidity (pH), when using a new combination of leaf or process types. Does Black Mammoth have the same impact on pH as more common Dark Air-Cured varieties? What happens when they are cooked into Cavendish? Will a tiny amount of Basma be detectable in a blend of otherwise dark, heavy, more alkaline leaf varieties?

In your own blending, you will often need to make small adjustments to my recipes, simply because some leaf properties are different from one crop to the next. Look on such adjustment as opportunities to improve your own intuition about what blends and ratios most suit your personal preferences. As with food recipes, pipe blend recipes can provide you with a solid *starting point* for your own blending explorations.

Processes discussed in my previous volume, such as Perique pressure-curing, Cavendish cooking, plug pressing, don't just add to your list of potential ingredients, they *multiply* your blending possibilities. The more tobacco varieties you have to start out with, the more fun you will have trying the various processes that you can apply to them to alter their bite or taste or aroma.

As with the previous volume, none of these new blends utilize flavorants or humectants. They are all about pure tobacco blends. Maintaining a smokable moisture level in pure tobacco—lacking humectants like propylene glycol or glycerin to keep them eternally squishy for commercial shelf life—depends on a relatively vapor-resistant container, and on your flicking a few drops of water into the container from your fingers, from time to time. Besides, humectants invariably diminish the burn of tobacco, and often alter the taste in unfavorable ways. As for flavorants, my preference is for tobacco flavor, in all its myriad nuances.

Some of the blends were created in "sets", even though they are listed in this volume alphabetically, by the blend name. For example, my "Frog" series consists of **Yellow Frog, Calico Frog, Black Frog, Top Frog, Peruvian Frog, Diamond Frog** and **High Desert Frog**. Another "set" is **Monarch** and **Red Admiral**, very similar blends with noticeable differences created by tiny adjustments in the blend ratios. There are other "sets", which are paired blends.

I decided to include a brief chapter on alternative leaf varieties that may give similar, though seldom identical, results to a variety listed a blend recipe. An example would be (Kentucky) Dark Air-Cured, which can be substituted by Small Stalk Black Mammoth, India Dark Air-Cured, Little Yellow, and others. Each of these varieties is classed as Dark Air-Cured, but each offers its own unique properties to a blend.

Blending one's own pipe tobacco is just a matter of re-categorizing pipe tobacco from "a thing that I buy" to "a thing that I make." Like an omelet or a pizza or a pot of bouillabaisse, how it comes into existence is a mystery

—until you re-categorize it. I believe that the reinforcement of creating your own pipe blends is not so much that it can taste as good as any commercial blend, but rather that it grants the person who blends it a sense of agency —of control over at least a tiny portion of the universe. (And then there is the little smile of recognizing the silliness of pipe tobacco mystique and marketing.)

Common Percentage vs. Parts per 16, for blending components

percent	parts per 16		percent	parts per 16
6.25	1		56.25	9
12.5	2		62.50	10
18.75	3		68.75	11
25.00	4		75.00	12
31.25	5		81.25	13
37.50	6		87.50	14
43.75	7		93.75	15
50.00	8		100.00	16

For any batch, you can simply measure by volume (tablespoons or cupfuls, etc.) instead of weight, so long as the shred of the various components is roughly similar. This typically introduces no more error than the variation of the very same leaf from season to season, crop to crop. For most of my repeat blending of the same blend components, I use tablespoons. When do I notice a difference, it is not due to the approximate blending, but to a sudden change in the source of a particular ingredient.

If you choose to measure the percentage of components by weight, keep in mind that you will need to stabilize the moisture content of each of the components to always be the same. Moisture content may vary with the very same ambient relative humidity, if the temperature differs from one measurement to the next.

A note about Cavendish:
Commercial "Cavendish", regardless of flavoring or absence thereof, is from a different universe than the many instances of Cavendish in my pipe blend recipes. The truly simple process of making your own Cavendish from pure, whole leaf tobacco (without humectants or flavored casings) is discussed in detail in the previous volume: *Blend Your Own Pipe Tobacco*. Learning to make Cavendish is similar to learning how to read—it opens so many doors that you never knew existed. I encourage you to give the processes a try. Making Cavendish of each variety that you have doubles your available blending ingredients [Yay!], *and the number of possible blends increases exponentially (with the square of the number of ingredients available)* [Wow!].

Making Latakia at Home

What is Latakia?

Latakia (the name of an ancient city on the Mediterranean coast of present-day Syria) is a specialty fire-cured tobacco popular in many pipe blend recipes. Historically, it was grown and created in the vicinity of Latakia. The firing of Latakia has mostly, if not entirely, ceased in Syria, and has in the last few decades been created on the island of Cyprus, though this production area now faces increasing challenges. Although specific Oriental tobacco varieties used for Latakia were named by authors during the late 19th century, and endlessly repeated by later tobacco "authorities", most of whom never visited the areas involved, my impression is that it has always been produced from Basma-type Oriental varieties, both in Syria and Cyprus. What makes Latakia unique is not the variety of the leaf, but the type of combustible materials used for firing it, and the duration of that firing—resulting in a nearly black leaf with an incense-like aroma. That it is made from Basma accounts for its low nicotine level.

All Basma type tobacco grown just about anywhere within the range of the former Ottoman Empire was grown in semi-arid conditions, without irrigation, without intentional fertilization, and planted closely-spaced (about 6 to 10 inches between plants). This produces stalks in the range of about 3 feet (1 meter) in height, with up to about 40 smallish leaves per stalk. (You can, of course, start with cured, commercial, whole-leaf Oriental tobacco, and fire it into Latakia.)

My initial attempts at making "Latakia" started with green leaf. That's okay, so long as the firing temps are kept quite quite low (below about 100°F) until the leaf has yellowed. Even after that, the temps must be kept below about 130°F for the duration of the firing process. This is similar to smoking foods such as meats and cheeses. My last attempt at "Latakia" production began with fully sun-cured leaf.

The smoking process itself is all about the materials that are burned to produce the smoke. Any Oriental tobacco, as well as any Virginia type tobacco, can probably be made into respectable "Latakia". That is to say, the firing materials dominate over any varietal differences in the tobacco. But it does need to be a variety that suitably sun-cures (i.e. Oriental or Virginia).

In contrast to Kentucky fire-cured leaf, which is generally fired over smoldering oak wood and oak sawdust, Latakia is fired over a (likely random and ever-changing) collection of woody materials native to the Mediterranean basin. These include the woody stems of many common, aromatic herbs, as well as scraps of Mediterranean pine and a Mediterranean live oak.   The aromas identifiable in commercial Latakia are similar to those in many types of

Trash can smoker in operation.

incense. (As an example, the smoldering wood of dried rosemary stems alone—not the leaves—is strikingly suggestive of the aroma of Latakia.)

While Kentucky fire-cured leaf is fired for a duration measured in days to two weeks, Latakia requires firing for a minimum of six weeks, before it even begins to suggest a black color. A firing of two to three months may be needed.

Latakia Smoke Materials Source	Correct +Fragrance	Unpleasant or -Not Right	Availability	Tested
Apple Wood		--		y
Ash Wood		--		y
Bay Leaf (*Laurus nobilis*) [not Indian Bay Leaf]	++		easy	y
Black Tea		---		y
Blackberry Cane (old, dried)	+	-		y
Cloves (whole)	+++		abundant	y
Coriander Seed	+	-		y
Forsythia Stem	++		abundant	y
Grape Vine (dried)	++		abundant	y
Gum Arabic		---		y
Hazel Wood		---		y
Hazelnut Shell	+	-		y
Hickory Wood		--		y
Honeysuckle [yellow] (*Lonicera flava*) Stem	+++		abundant	y
Honeysuckle [yellow] (*Lonicera flava*) Leaf				
Juniper Berries (from grocer)	+++		abundant	y
Lavender [English] Leaf	+	-	garden	y
Lavender [English] Stem	+		garden	y
Lilac (*Syringa vulgaris*) Leaf (dried brown)		--		y
Lilac (*Syringa vulgaris*) Wood	++		abundant	y
Maple Wood		--		y
Marjoram Leaf				
Marjoram Stem				
Mint Stem	+++		abundant	y
Oak Moss (*Evernia prunastri*)	+		abundant	y
Oak Wood		--		y
Oregano Leaf		---		y
Oregano Stem	+		abundant	y
Pine Needles, brown	+		abundant	y
Pine Wood	+	-	abundant	y
Pistachio Shells	+		expensive	y
Red Cedar [Eastern] (*Juniperus virginiana*)	+++		abundant	y
Rock Rose (Cistus ladanifer)				
Rosemary Leaf	+	--		y
Rosemary Stem	+++		abundant	y
Sage Leaf		--		y
Sage Stem		--		y
Sweet Gum seed pod	+++		abundant	y
Tears of Chios (mastic gum)	+++		rare	y
Thyme Leaf		--		y
Thyme Stem				
Xanthan Gum		---		y

Firing Materials:

My quest for identifying locally available firing materials suitable for making Latakia was guided by a simple test. Using the burner of an electric stove, I would place a tiny bit of material (stem or leaf or fragment) onto the burner, turn the heat to high, then smell the aroma of the smoke its combustion created. If it seemed like an aroma that might be compatible with Latakia, then I recorded it as such. This slow process of acquiring prospects, and testing their combustion aroma, one-by-one spanned several years. My results, which are purely subjective, are presented in accompanying chart. This approach will be of no value, unless you have already smelled Cyprus Latakia or Syrian Latakia.

does it smell bad? (lots of those)
does it smell wrong for Latakia? (e.g. hickory, oak, maple and apple smell "wrong")
does it offer nice aromas that may work well with Latakia? (a bunch of those)
does it shout out "Latakia"? (a rare few)

There were many surprises there. Mastic gum (tears of Chios) was perfect, while gum Arabic was awful. But then, brush from *Pistacia lentiscus* (mastic) is commonly used in Cyprus.

My Basic Steps:
1. Sun-cure an Oriental variety.
2. Suspend the cured leaves within a smoking container in such a manner that there is at least a tiny gap between each of the leaves.
3. Build a small fire at the bottom of the smoker.
4. Rest a foil pack containing selected firing materials on the burning coals. The foil should be perforated on the upper surface.
5. Repeat steps 3 and 4 two or three times each day, continuing until the leaves appear nearly black (~2 to 3 months).
6. Place the low-case, fired leaf into a vapor-proof bag, and seal.
7. Kiln at 128°F for 2 months.
8. Age for a further 1 to 2 years.

What You Get:
You will unquestionably end up with intensely smoky leaf. The degree to which it resembles Cyprian Latakia depends entirely on how closely your firing materials (quantities and ratios) approximate those used in Cyprus.

My "small fire", used for heating foil packs of selected herbs, spices, woods, was made from either bark-free pitch pine and white pine, or Eastern Red Cedar (which is actually a juniper, *Juniperus virginiana*, rather than a cedar). When available, I used dried lilac wood, which would have been preferable.

Nearly sun-cured Trabzon.

My random firing packs (the smoking materials) consisted of:
bay leaves (dried)
cloves (whole) as well as clove oil
Forsythia stems
grape vine clippings (dried)
honeysuckle stems
juniper berries
lavender, English, stems (dried)
lilac wood

mint stems (dried)
oregano stems (dried)
pine needles
pistachio shells
rosemary stems (dried)
sweet gum seed pods
Tears of Chios (mastic gum)

My final product is very dark brown to black, and smells of mild incense, but also smells a bit like a campfire. It's pleasant, but misses my target aroma. I attribute this to the pine wood and the red cedar (juniper) wood that I used. Perhaps an electric element used in place of a small fire could eliminate those woods. (Another alternative would be a propane/butane fueled backpacking stove with a "remote" fuel hose—so that the fuel canister can be positioned outside the smoker, with the foil packs of stems and herbs placed on its burner.) But the result is a mild, uniquely aromatic, fire-cured pipe blending ingredient. The method works, but depends entirely on the selection of combustion materials.

I will emphasize that the finished Latakia changes significantly with aging. And by that, I mean month by month, and year by year, continuing to become more subtle beyond 5 years of aging.

Using the inverted can lid to hold the leaf rack, I stacked and stuffed leaf onto each of the wires. The rack was then turned right side up, and suspended within the smoker can.

Wire leaf rack resting in the inverted lid, in order to "string" the leaf onto the individual wires.

Wire rack as it will hang within the can.

Aroma Thoughts:
On the "soapy" front, I once ordered some "Organic, unscented, hypoallergenic soap." When it arrived, I noted immediately that it smelled "soapy"—that is, it smelled like old fashion soap. The label touted its wonderfulness, but the ingredients listed "oil of rosemary." Unscented? Rosemary?

I emailed the vendor of the soap to inquire as to why my unscented soap was scented. His response was that, in the absence of chemical antioxidants to keep the soap from going rancid, rosemary has been used for centuries—since it contains natural antioxidants.

Sun-cured Trabzon leaf attached to the wire rack (upside-down from how it will hang).

Brinkmann smoker (fire in the base pan) and trash can with a grill thermometer. Holes are cut into the bottom of the trash can.

Latakia smells "soapy".
Rosemary stems turned into charcoal smell like Latakia.
Rosemary has long been used in preserving soap.

The aroma of charcoal produced from rosemary stems was so startlingly similar to the aroma of Latakia, that I got rather curious. I searched for an analysis of what is in rosemary oil. It turns out that it shares many of the same terpenes and other volatiles that are in mastic (Tears of Chios, which is dried sap from *Pistacia lentiscus*), and are common in many other evergreen trees (pines, junipers, etc.)

Here is my summary of the analysis of rosemary oil, followed by → a layman's hint of the general aroma:
α-Pinene 9.32% → pine
Camphene 5.07% → camphor
Limonene 3.19% → camphor / lemon
1,8-Cineole 37.75% → camphor
Camphor 18.13% → camphor
α-Terpineol 6.98% → forest like
Borneol 8.17% → camphor
Eugenol methyl ether 0.47% →clove
Eugenol 0.29% → clove

Cineole, camphor, pinene and borneol are the major constituents of rosemary oil, comprising about 38, 18, 9 and 8% of the oil respectively. And that does not consider the intensity of their aromas, such as from eugenol.

Historical Scraps:
BAT (British-American Tobacco) in 1964 states, regarding Cyprus Latakia, "The plants used mainly for fumigation are Cyprus Myrtle and Lentisk [Mastic tree]. Pine, Carob and the Scrub Oak used in Syria are not used though they grow in the vicinity." Yet, in 1984 BAT says this:

"some names of woods used in Cyprus, which mentions proper names and may be of use:
MASTIC - PISTACIA LENTISCUS: **90%**
MYRTLE - MYRTUS COMMUNIS ROMANA: 4 %
STONE PINE - PINUS PINEA PINUS PINASTER: 4 %
CYPRESS TREE - CYPRESSUS SEMPERVIRENS: 1%
KONISON- ?: 1%"

Some Home-Fired Latakia Caveats:

First of all, this prolonged, intense firing is time consuming. For the size of a batch that the average home grower will likely attempt, I believe the effort (though fun and educational, from a hobby standpoint) is not worth it. So long as you can purchase commercial Latakia, the ordeal of making your own is just too much.

A second issue is the campfire smell that will permeate your hair, skin, shoes and clothing each time you initiate another firing. You may not notice that smell, but others certainly will. At two firings a day, you are doomed to smell smoky (perhaps intensely smoky) for two straight months--minimum.

Each of us woud be making Latakia with different firing materials, each one of which contributes easily a dozen aroma components. I'm suspecting that so long as the collection of firing materials excludes certain strong, recognizable, incorrect components and includes certain strong, recognizable, essential components, that all the other odor variants tossed in there simply serve to "generalize" the overall aroma to a Latakia-like aroma. I can just about guarantee that in Cyprus, the exact materials and exact quantities of each differ from year to year, and even batch to batch.

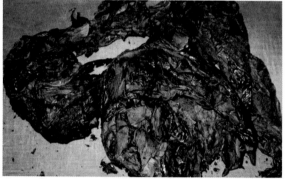

A small portion of the Trabzon Latakia batch, showing variations in color. It is still wadded-up from being stored stacked within a 10-inch wide poly-nylon bag for 2 years.

Trabzon Latakia closeup.

The batch of Trabzon leaf made in the previously shown photos yielded roughly 1¼ pounds of finished leaf. Although whole leaf Cyprus Latakia exhibits variations in color (ranging from pitch black to a medium brown), from one portion of a leaf to another, the color variations in my Trabzon Latakia were a little more common. I am certain that in both cases, the lighter color is due to that portion of a leaf being in contact with another leaf during the firing process. The ideal would be to allow a well-maintained space between the hanging leaves, so that the smoke exposure is equal over all the surfaces of each leaf.

Like all Latakia, the individual leaves, once fully fired and packed, are difficult to separate from one another. With both Cyprus Latakia as well as my Trabzon Latakia, I shred it by holding a clump of it onto the cutting board, while cutting it with my Kuhn Rikon 6-Inch kulu blade (which is no longer available). A chaveta with a section of Tygon tubing on the spine—for cushioning your palm—can work just as well. Kuhn Rikon does still offers a stainless, flat-bladed 6-inch Mezzaluna, which sells for about $16.00.

Mezzaluna

Corncob Pipe Repair

Repairing a Missouri Meerschaum *General* "second"

This is not a homemade pipe. But it does demonstrate a technique that I have used on a number of homemade pipes, especially those made of a cob or ash or fruit wood or even a corn stalk.

The MM *General* is a long, deep smoke. The bottom of the cob bowl remains cool for an entire bowl of tobacco. But its design is silly (if you don't have an aide constantly at your behest, who can hold it for you when you need to set it down). It is not a sitter, and will fit no pipe stand or pipe rest, unless you make one specifically to fit it. I use one of the few properly proportioned, empty tobacco tins that can keep it mostly upright.

My *General* was included among the 10 random pipes in a box of "seconds" that I purchased from MM a few years ago. I believe it (incorrectly) had a straight stem shoved into it when it arrived. Also, it arrived with a crack along the bowl rim. After close inspection, this crack appeared to extend down about 2/3 of the length of the bowl. I considered repairing it immediately, but could not convince myself that I could adequately close the hairline crack. So I smoked a dozen or two bowls of tobacco in it, to scorch and open the crack wide enough to admit some of my pipe spackle.

Interior crack and burn-through at the rim.

Runny spackle.

Exterior view of crack, and the thickening spackle.

Plaster of Paris (PofP) will shrink and crack as it dries. To prevent this,
I create an exactly 50:50 mixture of PofP [purchased from a home improvement store] and fine sand [purchased in the craft section of Walmart]. I have used this successfully as a fire-proof liner in my otherwise flamboyantly flammable corn stalk pipe, and that has held up well for a few years now. It is also ideal for repairing the interior bottom of a cob pipe that has begun to burn through. I've even used the PofP/sand spackle to repair a pipe made of real Meerschaum.

With this specific job, I mixed ½ level teaspoon of each dry ingredient. For spackling the inside of a pipe bowl, both the sides and rounded tips of a wooden Popsicle stick (craft stick) serve as a useful trowel. The quantity of water to add to the blended, dry PofP with sand is exactly less than the few drops that you do add. Always. But that's okay. A runnier mixture will penetrate cracks better, and it begins to set fairly quickly. You can mix this in the bottom of a cut-off paper or plastic cup, which can then be discarded afterwards.

With this cracked *General,* I began with a slightly runny spackle, which seeped its way into the defect. As the mixture became a little thicker, I added a second layer to the interior of the bowl, and freshened the bowl rim.

Spackle applied.   *Completed repair.*

The repair chore itself takes about 2 minutes, start to finish. What always takes me more time is retrieving the spackle ingredients from where I store them, and then returning them when I'm done.

Once fully set, I use a partially worn out cardboard emery board (nail file) to smooth the rim, and a rolled-up section of stiff sandpaper to lightly smooth the interior of the bowl.

Making a Simple Pipe Shank Tool

The handy rod-like element in a Czech pipe tool is often way too short for many of the longer pipe shanks, like those on Canadians.

I purchased this **14 gauge**, galvanized **steel** wire at the local hardware store. (100 feet of this wire is cheaper than all but the least expensive commercial pipe tools.) Having used aluminum wire for stringing tobacco, I was impressed with how stiff this steel wire felt.

I used the spark plug socket for creating the circular bend, and the small needle-nose pliers for the angled bends. It required quite a bit of effort to create the bends, so crud within a pipe shank is no match.

A shank tool should not have a sharp edge at the business end, so if one is created with the cutting process, it will need to be filed off. A 90° cut is ideal. An anvil and a hammer can remove any wiggles in the shaft.

The wire in the center of the circle provides some purchase for my fingers. You can sculpt a panda or a star ship, but it does need a shape that is convenient to hold. The length of the shaft should be only as long as the longest shank on any of your pipes. The long one shown here will make it through my longest bamboo shank on the corncob sitters that I make.

Wire Gauge vs. diameter in inches:
1/16" rod = 4/64"
14 gauge steel wire is 5/64"
12 gauge steel wire is 7/64"
1/8" rod = 8/64"

Easy Plug for Making Flake

My approach with forming the plug bypasses the need for a container and a press. I began by rolling a fat (~64 to 70 ring) cigar, using Lemon Virginia and still-soggy, whole leaf Perique as the filler, bound and wrapped in more Lemon Virginia. I then pressed it between two wood planks, using a hand-tightened clamp. (That's the same clamp I use for my Perique press.) This "plug" will simply be a cigar shape that has been flattened.

Pressing the cigar into a plug, using a screw clamp.

This "plug" was pressed for one week, tightening the clamp whenever possible. In order to slice the flake without unduly fracturing the binder and wrapper layers, I misted the exterior of the plug. I then sliced it into my "talus" flake. I use no casing.

End view, showing the pipe blend.

Fully pressed.

End view of finished plug.

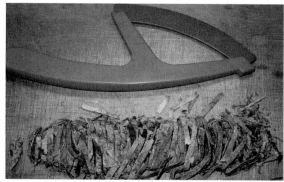

Plug sliced using a 6" kulu blade.

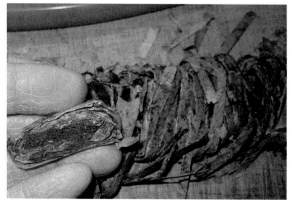

Sliced flake.

I allowed the sliced flake to dry on my back porch, in occasional sunlight, while resting on a seedling heat mat for about 24 yours.

Drying above a seedling heat mat.

Talus Flake

Birdseye Coins

The goal in rolling the "cigar" for birdseye coins is to nest color-contrasting ingredients in concentric layers, so that the cut flake (the coins) have an eye-like appearance. An additional challenge is to press the "cigar" to as round a cross-section as possible. This pressing requires some kind of form. I have used a large ring, single cigar box, shimmed on either side of the cigar, to keep it as more of a square than a flattened rectangle. A large ring size cigar mold can be used, if the rolling of the "cigar" is as dense and tight as possible. If you slice it with a single blade, the coins will flatten somewhat. Using a tuck cutter or double-guillotine cigar clipper may yield a rounder coin. Regardless, as the moist, pressed coins begin to dry, they will assume a more circular form. For a tiny, contrasting point in the center of each coin, you can include a tobacco stem at the very center.

Alternative Leaf Varieties in Blending: Categories

Unique Tobacco Varieties

There are well over 3000 unique, well characterized varieties of *Nicotiana tabacum*. Commercially available whole leaf numbers in the low dozens of varieties, plus their various stalk-levels (priming levels). If you grow your own tobacco, you likely cannot reasonably grow every currently existing variety in a single lifetime. And new varieties (typically with additional disease or pest resistance) are created continually.

Every unique variety brings something special to a pipe blend. I have grown more than 100 varieties over the years, including over two dozen different Oriental varieties. My pipe blends are sometimes centered on specific ingredients to which you may or may not have access. Given that no two crops of the very same variety are identical, and the existence of many *similar* varieties, you should have no difficulty producing wonderful blends using my recipes with alternative varieties. Since I consider all of my blend recipes to be merely a starting point from which you should make adjustments to your specific leaf and preferred tastes, you should enjoy the experimentation with alternatives. With many blend recipes, I have also included, in addition to the highly specific recipe, a second, "generic" or categorical recipe.

USDA Use Classes of Tobacco

During the second half of the 19th century, the US Department of Agriculture (USDA) classified tobacco varieties into groups based on their most common use in the then current marketplace. Some of those categories are somewhat useful today, though some are silly and meaningless.
- Burley
- Flue-cured
- Dark Air-cured
- Dark Fire-cured
- Maryland
- Cigar Filler
- Cigar Binder
- Cigar Wrapper
- Oriental
- Hungarian
- Primitive

Burley varieties are low in sugars, and air-cure to a unique aroma. But burley was often used in cigar manufacture in the US. Flue-cured varieties are typically Orinoco-derived varieties that are relatively high in sugars, and can therefore be successfully flue-cured. But many Oriental varieties (typically originating in the territories of the former Ottoman Empire) are also relatively high in sugars, and can also be successfully flue-cured.

Both dark air-cured and dark fire-cured varieties produce large, thick, sticky, high-nicotine leaves, and can be successfully cured either way. Separating them is simply an exercise in tobacco production geography and history, but is otherwise meaningless. By contrast, Hungarian varieties have only one attribute in common with one another: they were originally produced within the former Austro-Hungarian Empire. Again, simply a history lesson that is of little use today.

Useful Categories for Pipe Blending

Flue-cured tobacco (whether a "Virginia" type or an Oriental) produces smoke with a relatively low pH. That is to say, their smoke is *more* acidic. Too much acidity creates tongue bite toward the tip of the tongue. When a flue-cured variety is air-cured, rather than flue-cured, its smoke produces a somewhat higher pH: not as acidic.

Burley, Maryland, dark air-cured and all cigar types produce smoke with a higher pH. That is to say, their smoke is *more* alkaline. Too much alkalinity creates tongue bite toward the back of the tongue.

When the pH of the smoke is between the two extremes, what you might consider the Goldilocks zone, tongue bite simply vanishes. Cooking any variety of leaf into Cavendish moderates its pH, tending to bring it more toward the Goldilocks zone. Anaerobically pressure-curing any variety of leaf will always increase the pH of its smoke (more alkaline). So, in experimental blending, the proportions of each of these types of ingredients can be rationally adjusted toward a final blend in that bite-free, Goldilocks zone of smoke pH.

Cigar Leaf

I categorize cigar leaf into four fairly distinct groups:
- Caribbean-style cigar varieties (used for most commercial cigars today: Corojo, Criollo, Olor, Piloto Cubano, etc.) Most of these are widely grown throughout South America as well.
- Indonesian cigar varieties (Sumatra, Besuki, etc.)
- Broadleaf and seedleaf varieties (Pennsylvania, Ohio, Wisconsin and Connecticut types—though not Shade types)
- Little Dutch and Red cigar varieties (Little Dutch, Dutch Ohio, PA Red, Long Red)

Caribbean-style cigar varieties used in pipe blending often produce smoke that smells "like a cigar", though this can be softened by cooking that cigar leaf component into Cavendish. Indonesian cigar varieties, while having their own, unique aromas, are not as noticeably cigar-like in a pipe blend.

The broadleaf and seedleaf varieties are simply different in their aroma from Caribbean-style cigar varieties. Though still used to some extent in commercial cigars (CT Broadleaf, for example), they blend more readily into pipe blends. Though it is true that the Little Dutch and Red cigar varieties are indeed suitable for cigars, they don't shout "cigar", when used in a pipe blend.

Virginia or Flue-Cured

The term, "Virginia", is a categorical and historical name for tobacco that is flue-cured. The same is true for the term "bright tobacco". Most flue-cured varieties can be substituted for one another in a blend recipe, with the most significant determinant being the priming level (stalk position at which it grows). The lower leaf (lemon, bright) produces a sweeter leaf, and therefore more acidic smoke, when compared to upper leaf (Virginia red). When air-cured, the smoke of the leaf is noticeably less acidic (and less flavorful). Virginia varieties that are sun-cured will produce smoke that is more acidic and more flavorful than air-cured, but not as prominently as the smoke of flue-cured.

Oriental

There are dozens of Oriental varieties. For the majority, they are sweet and somewhat floral. Some, however, are what as known as semi-Orientals, often with larger leaves and with less distinctive Oriental character. All are traditionally sun-cured. I generally break them down into several groupings for blending:

- Basma-types, which include Xanthi, Yenidje, Ismir, Basma, Krumovgrad, etc., are among the most floral. Prilep (from North Macedonia) is derived from Basma, and though distinctive, can be loosely grouped here.
- Samsun-types (with a spade or heart-shaped, petiolate leaf) include Samsun, Bafra, Trabzon, and Katerini. These tend to produce an edgier smoke than the Basma types.
- Ox-tongue types are relatively long, narrow and pointed. These include Kanik, Shirazi, etc., and seem to be less floral, somewhat higher in nicotine, and produce smoke not quite as acidic as the Basma and Samsun types.

What does this mean for pipe blending? Perhaps not much. Substitutions from within one of the above categories of Oriental are most likely to come close to the specified ingredient. But for most pipe blending, only minor adjustments are enough to render any Oriental suitable for the Oriental component of a blend.

Burley and Maryland

The aroma of all burleys is distinctive. Maryland varieties lack that burley aroma. Beyond that, most Maryland types (Catterton, Keller, MD 609, etc.) can be used to substitute for burley in a pipe blend. Maryland smoke is often a bit less alkaline than that of burley. Both of these classes tend to be more hygroscopic than other tobacco classes, which means that they tend to attract and hold more moisture. Maryland is well know for soaking up added flavorants. Both of these make wonderful Cavendish. My favorite is Cavendish made from the upper leaf of burley (burley red tips).

General Guidelines for Variety Substitutions

If you are able to exactly duplicate the ingredients and proportions of any of my pipe blends, it will not be the same. There is practically no way around the variability in the annual crops and growing regions for the various tobacco varieties. As either an agricultural commodity or a personally cultivated crop, what you get from the land and the growing season and the curing season will always vary. So take heart if you need to make substitutes.

Your safest substitution choices will be using other varieties within the same type of leaf. As an example, any Basma type can make an excellent substitute for any other Basma type. Similarly, Long Red is a perfect substitute for Dutch Ohio. Any broadleaf or seedleaf variety will be very close to any other broadleaf or seedleaf variety.

Next best would be substitutions within the same general class of tobacco. For example, using Olor in place of PA Broadleaf will deliver a different flavor and aroma, but will be in the general range of what the blend intended. Using a similar priming level (seco for seco, viso for viso, etc.) will produce better results than using a wildly different priming level from that in the recipe (e.g. using ligero in place of seco).

Oriental can be used in place of flue-cured Virginia, but the acidity will be different, and will require adjustment by trial and error. But that sort of testing and re-formulating is really part of the fun of blending your own pipe tobacco.

A Word About Perique

Here, I am discussing pressure-cured perique, rather than the tobacco variety. Commercially purchased perique is likely to produce smoke that is considerably more alkaline than perique that you pressure-cure yourself. Your perique can be made from any tobacco variety, with the nicotine strength of the final perique being dictated by your choice of tobacco variety. So any blending recipe calling for perique can be made with either commercial or home-cured perique, but you will surely need to make at least minor adjustments in the proportions, in order to maintain a balanced acidity in the blend.

What is "Case"

A Confusing, Historical Term

This is a quite old tobacco term that vexes most people unfamiliar with its use. With regard to tobacco, it is a statement of its moisture content. "Out of case" describes tobacco that is so dry that it crumbles to fragments and dust when handled in any way. "In case" describes tobacco that contains a high enough moisture content that it can be easily handled, without damaging the leaf. With regard to users of whole leaf tobacco, and for those who grow, cure and finish tobacco, there are four general levels of case:

- **out of case**: very noisy, like dried autumn leaves, and crumbles when handled
- **low case**: much quieter, is mostly flexible, though it may crack slightly when folded
- **medium case**: sounds like thick vinyl, is entirely flexible, and has a moderate stretch
- **high case**: silent, feels somewhat moist, though not wet, is flexible and fully stretchy

In this usage, "case" should not be confused with "casing", which refers to the addition of liquids (often flavorings) to tobacco. It also has nothing to do with the concept of a container, as in, "packed in a case".

Tobacco can be stored out of case (totally dry), so long as it is protected from physical damage. When out of case, stored tobacco ages very little. Tobacco stored in low case will age properly, and not mold. Tobacco stored in medium or high case will promptly (within a few days to a few weeks) mold, and be ruined. (Above 122°F [50°C], mold cannot grow. So high case leaf within a well regulated tobacco kiln will not mold.)

Different varieties of tobacco, as well as different stalk levels of the same variety exhibit differing tendencies to draw in and hold moisture. This tendency to draw and hold moisture is its hygroscopic tendency. Upper leaf or thicker leaf is usually more hygroscopic than lower or thinner leaf. Stems are usually more hygroscopic than the leaf lamina. Burley and Maryland varieties are often more hygroscopic than other varieties.

For storage of leaf, its sound and feel should guide the determination of case. While 60% relative humidity (RH) is usually safe, and usually maintains low case, this is not true of all leaf. Also, RH changes significantly with a change in temperature. Just get accustomed to touching and listening to the leaf to determine case. Always store tobacco in relatively stable temperatures.

Why does stable temperature matter? If one side of a container is colder than the other side, then the closed container will function like a heat pump, with moisture gradually evaporating from the warmer side, and condensing on the cooler side. The result is eventually mold in the leaf on the cooler side.

The level of case can be lowered by exposing the leaf to drier conditions, then sealing it when it seems to be in low case. The level of case can be raised by exposing it to more humid conditions, or by lightly misting it with non-chlorinated water. As an example of misting, a one pound bag of leaf that is out of case can easily absorb 4 to 6 sprays of water from a typical spray bottle. Then it should be sealed overnight or for a few days, in order to evenly distribute the moisture.

With minimal practice, determining and adjusting the case of tobacco leaf becomes intuitive. No instrumentation required.

World's Ugliest Pipe

A Bad Idea from the Start

Bowl made from the buttress roots of a Boone County Corn stalk.

This sustainably produced wonder is manufactured from the very bottom of a corn stalk. It retains all the buttress roots. The shank is made from telescoping bamboo, with a Vulcanite bit. A fire-proof, 50:50 spackle mixture of plaster of Paris and fine sand lines the tobacco chamber.

It does not stand. It fits no known pipe stand. It is impossible to hold by the bowl. It was not only ugly, but distressing to smoke. A pipe should encourage relaxation. This one seemed to inspire horror. It seemed like a good idea at the time.

As a further discouragement, each and every root seemed to contain at least one tiny weevil that eventually ate its way to the root tip, leaving an air leak, along with a tiny pile of "sawdust" beneath the pipe. I suppose a week in a tobacco kiln would have eliminated the weevil problem from the start. But that could hardly remedy all of this pipe's issues. After a few weeks, I salvaged the stem and bit, and tossed the pipe bowl into the trash.

A close-up of the pipe bowl.

Specialty Yeast Perique: Beerique

by **Steven Farmer** (Fair Trade Tobacco Forum member @*GreenDragon*)

Overview

I love the depth of flavor and bite mitigating properties of perique tobacco in my pipe mixes. I also like to experiment and add variety to my blends, so I decided to make a few batches of house perique following the methods found on the forum; wet a batch of whole leaf tobacco, pack it tightly, and place in a vessel with a weight on top to compress the tobacco and keep it submerged below the surface of the expressed liquid. This method works well and makes fine homemade perique. However, there are two aspects of this technique that I do not care for; it takes several months to complete, and it can be quite smelly (think barnyard), particularly at first. This is caused by the presence of coliform bacteria that are endemic on the leaf. The fruity aromas and character of perique develop over time as yeast, specifically *Pichia anomala* (the randomly ubiquitous yeast responsible for the characteristic transformation of anaerobic pressure-curing in the Perique process), begin to slowly out-compete the bacteria, and take over the fermentation.

Figure 1: Starting the yeast.

The Yeast

Pichia anomala is a slow growing yeast, and difficult to culture for the home grower. However, what if I used a closely related yeast that is easy to obtain and grows quickly? *Saccharomyces cerevisiae* (brewer's yeast) fit the bill; easy to obtain and easy to culture. Starting with a concentrated yeast culture should prevent coliform bacteria from taking hold, eliminating the odorous phase of the process. So I purchased a variety of yeast from a brewing supply store and started my experiment.

The Process

1. Boil a cup of water plus one teaspoon sugar in a quart mason jar in the microwave for two minutes to sterilize the media. Immediately add the lid as soon as boiling is complete. Set aside to cool. When cooled to room temperature, add a packet of dry brewers' yeast to the jar, and replace the lid. Shake to dissolve the yeast and oxygenate the water. Loosen lid to allow gas to escape. Let ferment for 12-24 hours (figure 1).

2. Tightly pack whole leaf tobacco into a mason jar and add your yeast mixture. There should be just enough liquid to cover the packed leaf in the jar (figure 2). Loosely apply the lid, and set the jar in a bowl or tray to catch any overflow from the fermentation (figure 3). Let ferment for two weeks.

3. Remove the tobacco from the jar and spread out to dry. (figure 4) When it is just slightly moist, pack into a container and apply pressure for another two to four weeks. The easiest way I have found is to pack the tobacco into a quart freezer bag, place between two boards and stack weights on top. For the batch I made for this book, I used a cigar box press in a vise (figure 5).

4. Once pressing is complete the tobacco is ready to shred and dry for storage (figure 6).

Figure 2: Packing the leaf.

Figure 3: Initial fermentation (at room temperature).

Figure 4: Airing the leaf after two weeks.

Figure 5: Box press for continued fermentation.

Figure 6: Shredding the finished Beerique.

Variations

Experiment with different tobaccos and yeast varieties. For example, I've used ale yeast and red wine yeast with multiple varieties of tobacco such as dark air, Maryland, Virginia, etc. Each produced unique but delicious batches of house perique.

Why Beerique? I made my first batch using ale yeast, as I had it on hand. So I christened my creation "Beerique"!

[See Perk Up (using beer yeast Beerique) and Wine Dark Sea (using red wine Beerique) Blends]

Blend	Flue-cured	Oriental	Burley	Dark	Cigar	Cavendish	Perique	Latakia	MD	Other
1918						X				
Akron	X					X	X	X		
Altiplano	X		X	X		X	X		X	
American Cream	X			X						
Artifact	X	X	X							
Assyrian Dream		X		X						
Babies Bottoms	X			X		X				
Balkan Gold	X	X		X				X		
Beethoven's Fifth	X	X		X						
Big And Bold		X	X			X		X		
Big Yellow	X	X		X		X				
Bit of Red	X				X	X				
Black Bridge	X	X	X	X		X				
Black Frog	X				X		X	X		
Bronze Sky		X		X	X	X				
Brown Dwarf		X	X			X				
Burley With a Bite		X	X							
Calico Frog	X						X	X		
Carnotaurus Tail		X		X		X	X			
Christmas 2019	X	X		X		X			X	
Christmas 2021		X		X		X				X
Chuck Wills Widow	X	X			X			X	X	
Circle Limit III	X	X		X		X		X		
Circle Limit IV	X	X		X		X		X		
Citadelle	X	X					X			
Contrarian		X					X			
Corridor		X	X			X	X			
Countryside	X	X				X	X	X		
Cumbria	X	X	X			X	X	X		
Curiosity	X	X	X				X			
Debatable Lands	X	X				X	X			
Delta Bird's Eye	X	X	X	X		X	X			
Devil Eyed Frog	X		X	X		X	X			
Diamond Frog	X	X				X	X			

Blend	Flue-cured	Oriental	Burley	Dark	Cigar	Cavendish	Perique	Latakia	MD	Other
Dune Blend		X					X			
Early Morning Smoke		X				X	X			
Earth Rise	X						X			
Exmoor	X	X	X	X			X			
Forest Road	X	X	X			X				
Gentle On My Mine	X				X	X			X	
Golden Frog		X		X						
Greenbrier Two-Tone	X		X			X				
High Desert Frog		X			X	X				
Hubble Bubble		X		X		X				
Jaipur	X	X		X						
Just Walking Home	X	X	X	X		X	X			X
Karpas		X	X	X						
Lake Bled	X	X	X	X		X	X			
Lake Shkodra		X		X						
Long Red CAVEndish	X				X	X	X			
Marudnik		X		X						
Monarch		X	X			X				
Moonrise	X					X	X			
Noctilucent Knowlton	X				X	X				X
Old Guy	X	X				X	X			
Pearl of Shibam 2nd Edition	X	X					X	X		
Peruvian Frog	X	X			X	X				
Playful Mammoth		X		X		X		X		
Ptarmigan Hiding	X	X		X		X	X			
Ptarmigan Summer	X	X	X	X		X				
Punta Ventana 2020		X	X			X	X			
Raggedy Owl	X	X		X		X	X			
Red Admiral		X	X			X				
Red Caboose	X		X		X	X				
Red Train	X		X			X				
Reflection	X	X	X	X						
Sailing to Trabzon	X	X					X	X		
Shades of Dark	X			X	X	X				

Blend	Flue-cured	Oriental	Burley	Dark	Cigar	Cavendish	Perique	Latakia	MD	Other
Shinumo						X			X	
Silver Lining	X		X			X				X
Skree	X						X			
Smaug		X		X				X		
Smoky Man		X		X		X		X		
Sultan Qaboos	X	X	X	X		X				
Sunday Afternoon	X		X							
Sunset	X			X		X				
Sunspot	X			X		X				
Super Blood Wolf Moon Eclipse 2	X		X			X		X		
Takin a Break		X		X	X	X	X			
Talus	X						X			
Tegu	X						X			
Tenere	X	X	X	X		X				
The Barn	X	X	X					X		
Three Cavs	X		X			X			X	
Three Zebras		X				X		X		
Top Frog	X	X					X			
Typhoon	X	X		X		X				
Whale Foot		X		X	X	X				
Wine Dark Sea		X				X	X			X
Winter Ptarmigan	X	X		X		X	X			
Yellow Frog		X					X	X	X	
Zeus	X	X				X	X	X	X	

This grid lists each of the pipe blends alphabetically. An 'X' in a column indicates that at least one of the ingredients comes from the indicated class. If "Cavendish" is indicated, then at least one of those ingredients has been cooked into Cavendish.

1918: This tastes exactly like 104 year old pipe tobacco. Maybe. No need to wear a high, starched collar or a bow-tie in order to smoke it. A face mask may be required. There was no color back then.

Seriously, I expected the nicotine to be quite high, but it comes out in the medium-to-full range, with a wonderful Burley aroma. It's a robust, enjoyable smoke. Both my straight burley and my burley Cavendish are burley red tip (probably TN 89, and from the upper stalk positions). You can, of course use a milder burley or leaf from lower on the stalk.

If you smoke a bowl of 1918 after smoking a cigar, the pH jolt (that accompanies flue-cured or Oriental containing blends, following a cigar) is not there. Just a smooth pipe smoking experience.

1918
- Burley Cavendish 2/3
- Burley Red Tip 1/3

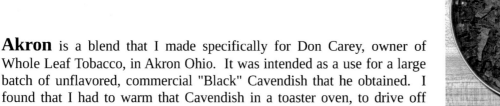

Akron is a blend that I made specifically for Don Carey, owner of Whole Leaf Tobacco, in Akron Ohio. It was intended as a use for a large batch of unflavored, commercial "Black" Cavendish that he obtained. I found that I had to warm that Cavendish in a toaster oven, to drive off much of the propylene glycol that the Cavendish contained, in order to use it for blending. So the "Cavendish" referenced in the blend recipe is generic.

The Navy's USS Akron, launched in 1931, was the very first flying aircraft carrier, and the largest helium ship ever built. In 1933, of the coast of New Jersey, while enveloped in a bank of fog, the ship encountered a severe lightening storm, with violent downdrafts, and was destroyed.

Akron
- Cavendish 43.75% (7 parts per 16)
- Red Virginia Flue-Cured 43.75% (7 parts per 16)
- Latakia 6.25% (1 part per 16)
- Perique 6.25% (1 part per 16)

Altiplano: This odd blend mirrors the intense weather often seen on Bolivia's Altiplano, the high Andes plateau, where you can encounter scorching heat, high winds, rain storms, freezing temperatures and blizzards—all in the same day. To draw a different metaphor, this blend might be considered the 90% cocoa bar of the pipe tobacco world.

It is rich and deeply flavorful, while offering zero tongue bite. Nicotine is full. Room note? I shudder to imagine. The greatest surprise is that such an off the wall blend is delicious. It may be rather close to the (somewhat "Periqued") twist rope tobacco sold in the region.

If you're not so sure, then make a mini batch of 1: 1: 1.5: 0.5 tablespoons. Surely you can spare 4 tablespoons of tobacco to transport yourself to the Altiplano. [Carry along gloves, a jacket, and a waterproof card with your next of kin information.]

Altiplano
- Dark Air Cavendish 25% (4 parts per 16)
- Maryland Cavendish 25% (4 parts per 16)
- Burley Cavendish 37.5% (6 parts per 16)
- Virginia Bright 12.5% (2 parts per 16)

Artifact: If you were to find a well preserved sample of a pipe tobacco blend within the chambers of a Mayan pyramid, it might taste a bit like this: dry, almost dusty, with a full-bodied "pure tobacco" aroma and a generous load of nicotine. (Upper leaf from a Virginia variety that has been sun-cured, if you have produced some, might be more true to the notion.) There is no tongue bite; no ceremonial hallucinations.

I think the creature in this image is depicted closing its eyes, while it puffs out a draw of delicious tobacco smoke. The relatively narrow flavor profile is mostly that of burley, with the bite removed.

Artifact
- Burley Red Tip 50% (8 parts per 16)
- Virginia Red Flue-cured 37.5% (6 parts per 16)
- Basma 12.5% (2 parts per 16)

Artifactoid
- Burley 50% (8 parts per 16)
- Virginia Flue-cured 37.5% (6 parts per 16)
- Oriental 12.5% (2 parts per 16)

American Cream: As you can see from the simplicity of this blend, you use a small proportion of Dark Air-Cured to balance the pH of its single other—but major—component. American Cream delivers horsepower. The flue-cured Lemon of American Cream is loud, and makes its presence known. The Dark Air-Cured eliminates tongue bite, and alters the overall aroma, increasing its complexity. Curiously, these ratios don't work as well with Perique replacing the Dark Air-Cured.

If I were to suggest a time-of-day rating for this blend, American Cream is more of a mid-day smoke.

American Cream
- Flue-cured Virginia Lemon 81.25% (13 parts per 16)
- Dark Air-Cured 18.75% (3 parts per 16)

Assyrian Dream: As you can see from the simplicity of this blend as well, it uses a small proportion of Dark Air-Cured to balance the pH of its single other—but major--component. The Basma —I used WLT Stacked Basma—of Assyrian Dream remains meek and subdued, like an ancient shard of text. (Is it a monthly bill from Sumer Electric Co-op, or maybe a used ticket stub from Nineveh Cinema?). The Dark Air-Cured eliminates tongue bite, and alters the overall aroma, increasing its complexity. Curiously, these ratios don't work as well with Perique replacing the Dark Air-Cured.

If I were to suggest a time-of-day rating for this blend, I would say that Assyrian Dream is a first pipe of the day. Assyrian is wonderful in the morning, but by late afternoon, after meals and other tobacco have left their marks on my taste buds, Assyrian tastes like nobody is home.

Assyrian Dream
- Basma 87.5% (14 parts per 16)
- Dark Air-Cured 12.5% (2 parts per 16)

Babies' Bottoms: [Photo: David W. Cerny] This is a rich, smooth, burley blend. Full smoke. Medium-to-full nicotine. No bite. Although I have used One Sucker *ligero* as the burley variety, you should be able to come close with any variety of burley upper leaf or dark air-cured. If you have a tobacco kiln, you can approximate the Virginia Double Bright by kilning Virginia lemon for a few weeks.

Babies' Bottoms
- Virginia Double Bright 50%
- One Sucker ligero Cavendish 37.5%
- One Sucker ligero 12.5%

Baby-ish Bottoms
Virginia Bright 50%
Dark Air-cured Cavendish 37.5%
Burley 12.5%

Balkan Gold: [Photo: Field Museum.] This is a mild (25%) Latakia, English-style blend that uses Virginia Double-Bright as its only Virginia, which is a bit higher in nicotine and less acidic than Lemon Virginia or standard Virginia Bright. There is only a taste of Basma as its Oriental. Little Yellow is a unique dark air-cured variety that typically cures out to a deep, orange-brown, rather than the dark brown of most dark air-cured varieties. Little Yellow also offers a rounder, somewhat less intense flavor, when compared to other dark air-cured leaf.

As blended, the Latakia is soft but noticeable, the nicotine moderate, and the aroma full and well rounded.

Little Yellow is not sold as commercial leaf. To obtain it, you will have to grow it yourself. As a dark air-cured variety, it air-cures easily. (It also makes a unique Cavendish, for other blends.)

Balkan Gold
- VA Double-Bright 50% (8 parts per 16)
- Latakia 25.00% (4 parts per 16)
- Basma 12.5% (2 part per 16)
- Little Yellow 12.5% (2 part per 16)

Balkan Gold-ish
- VA Flue-cured 50% (8 parts per 16)
- Latakia 25.00% (4 parts per 16)
- Oriental 12.5% (2 part per 16)
- Dark Air-Cured 12.5% (2 part per 16)

Beethoven's Fifth Symphony is brilliant and dark, with interludes of sunlight. Double-Bright is flue-cured Virginia that, after the flue-curing is complete, is subjected to prolonged heating, similar to what I've achieved by kilning Virginia Lemon that was already flue-cured. The result is less acidity, and a somewhat rounder (not as crisp) aroma.

The Dark Air-Cured dose in this blend is generous, yielding a somewhat full nicotine level. The Basma restores some of the missing acidity, giving the overall blend a splash of light. I consider this a mid to late-day blend.

Beethoven's Fifth
- VA Double-Bright 52.25% (9 parts per 16)
- Dark Air-Cured 25.00% (4 parts per 16)
- Basma 18.75% (3 part per 16)

Big & Bold needs little explanation. Don't argue with the hippo. At 62.5%, the Latakia is about as high a concentration as you can blend without needing to prevent it from separating out, by pressing it into a press-cake. Even for most Latakia lovers, this is a late-day smoke—perhaps a final pipe for the evening. For the Latakia novice, look into the Hippo's eyes. He means business.

Although the aroma of Latakia can be intense, its nicotine is relatively low, since it is made from Basma-type Oriental leaf. But the smoky intensity will give the surface of your tongue a workout.

Big & Bold
- Latakia 62.50% (10 parts per 16)
- Burley Cavendish 25.00% (4 parts per 16)
- Oriental 12.50% (2 parts per 16)

Big Yellow features the genuinely unique, dark air-cured variety named Little Yellow, both straight and as Cavendish. Little Yellow tends to cure to a yellow-brown, rather than the dark brown of most other dark air-cured varieties. Its taste and aroma are broader, rounder, and not quite as intense as its cousins.

For balance, the Orientals and Lemon Virginia provide enough acidity to the smoke to lend it a slight bite. Katerini is in the same family as Samsun, Bafra and Trabzon. So it is a bit darker and mellower than the Basma types.

Visually, most of the darker colors in this blend are from the Little Yellow and its Cavendish incarnation. Nicotine is full. Burn is excellent. I find it to be a tasty late day smoke.

Big Yellow
- Little Yellow 18.75% (3 parts per 16)
- Little Yellow Cavendish 25.00% (4 parts per 16)
- Katerini 18.75% (3 parts per 16)
- Basma 18.75% (3 parts per 16)
- Lemon VA 18.75% (3 parts per 16)

Big Yellow

Bit of Red: More than a bit. This simple blend leans heavily on my Long Red Cavendish. It will likely come out similar with PA Red, Little Dutch and Dutch Ohio (all cooked into Cavendish), but not so similar if made using the broadleaf/seedleaf Pennsylvania varieties. The pouch aroma is subdued. Its aroma is not cigar-like, but instead more like a kinder, gentler Dark Air-Cured blend pouch aroma. Nicotine load is dependent on the priming level of the Long Red that was chosen for the Cavendish. With my particular batch, the smoke is smooth, warm and seemingly mild, but the nicotine sneaks up silently to medium-to-full, without warning.

Bit of Red
- Long Red Cavendish 68.75%
    (11 parts per 16)
- VA Flue-cured Cavendish 31.25%
    (5 parts per 16)

Black Bridge: This Oriental and Cavendish blend is the product of successive, minor modifications and trials of my original Edinburgh blend. The combination of Cavendish varieties adjusts the pH balance to a happy value.

The pouch aroma of Black Bridge presents a bright, slightly "sour" aroma of Basma. When lit, the combination of burley Cavendish and Dark Air-cured Cavendish perform an excellent job of minimizing the tongue bite that would be associated with so much Basma, in the absence of Perique. Nicotine is on the robust side of medium. Overall, this seems to be a satisfying, enjoyable blend for the second half of the day.

Black Bridge
- Basma 50%
- Burley Cavendish 30%
- Dark Air-cured Cavendish 10%
- VA Bright Cavendish 10%

Black Frog: A robust Balkan blend.

Black Frog
- Latakia 43.5 % (7 parts per 16)
- Virginia Bright 37.5% (6 parts per 16)
- Perique 18.75% (3 parts per 16)

Bronze Sky

Of the dozens of different Oriental varieties I have grown and sampled, Trabzon seems to carry the heaviest weight. Although in the same family as Bafra, Katerini and Samsun (all with petiolate leaves), the Trabzon that I have grown has been somewhat higher in nicotine, and sun-cures to a darker color. Its productivity is high, even when closely planted, and it sun-cures on the stalk quite readily. Trabzon does offer a subtle floral aroma.

Of the cigar varieties that I have cooked into Cavendish, Long Red (along with PA Red, Dutch Ohio, Little Dutch and PA broadleaf varieties—like Lancaster and Glessnor) seems to lose its "cigar" aroma more thoroughly than Caribbean cigar varieties as a Cavendish. The Cavendish process also moves cigar leaf acidity slightly away from the alkaline end of the pH scale, meaning that its proportion can be increased in a blend, without blowing you away with nicotine absorption.

Bronze Sky has no white puffy clouds. It is medium-to-full in nicotine, and offers deep aromas. There is a light, floral overtone that I can detect only when I first light it. Bronze Sky's largest ingredient is Dark Air-Cured, but also cooked into Cavendish, which softens its impact quite a bit. The Dark Air Cavendish aroma dominates.

This bronze map of the sky (known as the Nebra Sky Disc) is thought to be about 3600 years old. It marks the solstices and positions of certain stars.

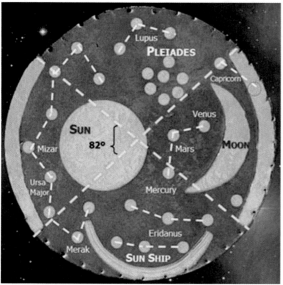

Bronze Sky
- Dark Air-Cured Cavendish 43.75% (7 parts per 16)
- Trabzon 37.5% (6 parts per 16)
- Long Red Cavendish 18.75% (3 parts per 16)

Bronze Sky value-brand generic
- Dark Air-Cured Cavendish 43.75% (7 parts per 16)
- Oriental 37.5% (6 parts per 16)
- Cigar leaf Cavendish 18.75% (3 parts per 16)

[Image: Stellar House Publishing]

A **Brown Dwarf** is a dud of a star—a disappointment. It forms all on its own, just like our Sun, but it just doesn't have what it takes to initiate fusion of hydrogen. It's too runty. Not enough mass. Instead, it bumbles along. A brown dwarf can't even emit visible light—only infrared. So they are not "brown", but infrared. *[They are not "ultra-cool" dwarfs, since, as everyone knows, tiny stellar objects cooler than 3092°F (1,700°C) must be brown dwarfs, while those hotter than 4,400°F (2,400°C) must be stars.]* When the Webb space telescope (an infrared-only telescope!) becomes operational, maybe we can actually see them clearly. In the mean time, just light up a bowl of this simple blend.

This is a medium-to-full bodied blend for burley lovers. The dominant pouch aroma is from the Burley Red Tip Cavendish. And the burley Cavendish provides much of the nicotine. The role of the Trabzon is to add a sharper edge, and lower the pH (acidity) from that of the burley Cavendish. Nothing light. Nothing bright. Room note is burley, burley and burley. Trabzon is in the same group of petiolate Orientals as Bafra, Katerini and Samsun, so those could easily substitute. Burley Red Tip is harvested from the upper leaves of the stalk. (You might consider the Red Tip the brown dwarf of this blend.) Using other burley leaf may require adjusting the proportions. Substituting a "brighter" Oriental, such as WLT Stacked Basma, for 2/3 of the Oriental provides a gentle approach to broadening the flavor profile. Using all stacked Basma for the Oriental component causes tongue bite.

Brown Dwarf
- Burley Red Tip Cavendish 50%
- Trabzon 50%

Infrared Dwarf
- Burley Cavendish 50%
- Oriental 50%

Burley with a Bite:

The name of this blend is a play off of Lane, Ltd. "Burley Without Bite". And indeed, there is a mild bite to this blend. Nicotine is medium to full. Burn is excellent. The smoke is full and rich, and ideal for later in the day.

Burley with a Bite
- Burley Red Tip 50%
- Basma 50%

House Blend Burley with a Bite
- Burley 50%
- Oriental 50%

[art by Jorge A. Gonzalez]

Burley with a Bite

BONUS BLEND

Burrowing Owl: This mild and tasty blend is primarily air-cured Maryland (I used MD 609 that I kilned), with a sprinkle each of Basma and Latakia. Easy to blend; easy to smoke. Since my MD 609 crop was stalk-cured, and not separated by stalk-level, this is a random blend of lower, mid-stalk and upper-stalk Maryland leaf.

Nicotine is a slight notch below medium. Lights and burns well. There is no tongue bite. Latakia is soft, floating in the background, although it presents the most distinctive smoke aroma of the three ingredients.

Burrowing Owl
- Maryland 75% (12 parts per 16)
- Basma 12.5% (2 parts per 16)
- Latakia 12.5% (2 parts per 16)

Calico Frog: A mild Balkan blend with full Perique.

Calico Frog
- Latakia 18.75 %
- Virginia Bright 43.75%
- Perique 37.50%

Calico Frog

Carnotaurus Tail:

Dino butt. Sounds enticing. Just watch out for that tail! While the Black Mammoth (a dark air-cured variety) Cavendish component can be made from any dark air-cured variety, the Black Mammoth is particularly potent and aromatic. Düzce is a Turkish Oriental variety, and can be replace by any Basma-type Oriental.

Nicotine is quite full. This is one of the few blends that I can rate for room note: whew! Taste and aroma are rich and satisfying. It's just a tail, so no bite. But that tail carries a wallop. I would consider this blend for a final bowl of the evening.

Carnotaurus Tail
- Black Mammoth Cavendish 50%
- Dark Air-cured 12.5%
- Düzce 37.5%

Carnotaurus Tail

Black Mammoth Cavendish 50%
Dark Air-cured 12.5%
Düzce 37.5%

art: Jake Baardse

BONUS BLEND

Chillingham: *"White as snow, with sinewy frames, a fierce temperament and vast horns that curve menacingly into jet-black tips, these are no ordinary oxen. Among the last remaining wild cattle in the world, they retain a primeval character. They are also some of the rarest animals on the planet; currently numbering around 130, they are far fewer in number than giant pandas, Siberian tigers or mountain gorillas."*
[BBC 16 SEP 2021]

This pipe blend, despite its heavy load of Cavendish, has a fierce temperament, though no horns. Unlike the Greenbriar Two-Tone blend, which is simply half and half burley Cavendish and VA Bright Cavendish, this one uses Cavendish made with upper leaf of both burley and VA flue-cured. Its nicotine is substantial, and requires taming with a sweet, Basma-type Oriental, in this case, Krumovgrad, though any Basma-type will do. It is still a hefty smoke (perhaps harboring a touch of Siberian tiger).

Chillingham
- Krumovgrad 18.75%
- Burley Red Tip Cavendish 37.5%
- Flue-cured Virginia Red Cavendish 43.75%

Chillingham

Christmas 2019: My 2019 Christmas Blend is free of cinnamon, allspice and other Far Eastern herbs and spices. It's just tobacco. This smooth blend provides a medium-to-full nicotine level, with no single component standing out. It also lacks both Perique and Latakia, the room notes of which have been accused of interfering with the boreal forest scents of traditional holiday decorations.

Christmas Blend 2019
- Virginia Red 62.50%
- Maryland Cavendish 12.50%
- Basma 18.75%
- Dark Air 6.25%

Christmas 2021: Like a gift from a relative or friend or co-worker, your "frozen sucker" Cavendish could end up being anything. Maybe a fidget toy. Maybe an ugly sweater. "Thank you, Nana. I love the sweater you made for me. That must have taken a long time." [Notice that the sweater sleeves are the perfect length for dinosaur arms.]

If you don't have "frozen sucker" leaf to make into Cavendish, then soothe your disappointment by making up for it with more dark air-cured Cavendish (or Cavendish made from any random or mystery leaf). My specific formula used WLT stacked Basma, mixed "frozen sucker" leaf Cavendish and One Sucker ligero Cavendish.

After shredding and blending, the tobacco was placed into a Ziploc freezer bag and simply pressed between two boards in a screw clamp. (The weight of Santa's sleigh was insufficient, so I estimated the bite force of a T-Rex.) The blend was pressed for about 2 weeks, then rubbed out.

Christmas 2021
- Oriental 62.5%
- Frozen Sucker Cavendish 18.75%
- Dark Air-Cured Cavendish 18.75%

Ugly Sweater 2021
- Merry and Bright 62.5%
- Random and Mild 18.75%
- Any Cavendish Visible in Twinkling, Multi-colored Lights 18.75%

Chuck Wills Widow: A whopping dose of flue-cured Virginia Red, balanced with cigar leaf (Nicaragua, if you dare) and Maryland.

Chuck-Wills Widow
- Latakia 18.75% (3 parts per 16)
- Maryland 12.5% (2 parts per 16)
- Oriental 12.5% (2 parts per 16)
- Cigar leaf viso 12.5% (2 parts per 16)
- Virginia Red 43.75% (7 parts per 16)

Circle Limit III: Exercise: Observe that each white arc is followed by flying fish of a single color. Each nexus is intersected by flying fish of three colors, yet there are four colors of flying fish.

This is a kinder, gentler approach to the recipe I used for Circle Limit IV. Circle Limit III offers a medium dose of Latakia, that stands out more than the percentage would suggest, in the absence of Perique aromas. Despite being half Lemon and Basma, I really don't sense a sweetness. The Dark-air Cavendish still ramps up the nicotine. I would consider it an "upper-medium" English blend.

Circle Limit III
- Latakia 37.5% (6 parts per 16)
- Dark-air Cavendish 12.5% (2 parts per 16)
- Lemon Virginia 31.25% (5 parts per 16)
- Basma 18.75% (3 parts per 16)

Exercise: Observe that each white arc is followed by flying fish of a single color. Each nexus is intersected by flying fish of three colors, yet there are four colors of flying fish.

Art for both of these is by the Dutch graphic artist, M.C. Escher (1959 and 1941, respectively). I encourage you to explore (Google) his various books of mind-bending art.

Circle Limit IV: This blend offers both a full aroma and a full taste. Nicotine is medium-to-full. The Latakia is heavy, but not super-high. I believe this would drag you down into the pit, if you use this much Dark Air-Cured that has not been transformed first into Cavendish. I suspect that the Cavendish process lowers the pH of its smoke a bit, presenting less of a nicotine hit. While the rich Latakia always adds a tingle to your tongue, the overall balance of the blend also contributes a tang. (Pay no attention to any bat wings that may appear. It's all angels.)

Circle Limit IV
- Latakia 50%
- Dark Air-Cured Cavendish 18.75%
- Flue-cured Lemon Virginia 12.5%
- Stacked Basma 18.75%

Citadelle: A Virginia / Perique / Oriental Blend

The pouch aroma is mild and slightly floral (from the Samsun). It lights easily and burns well. There is no bite, because of the 5:3 Bright to Perique ratio. The smoke aroma is mellow, with an undercurrent of Perique. Nicotine is mild to medium.

Citadelle
- Flue-Cured Virginia ~41.7%
- Oriental (I used Samsun) ~33.3%
- Perique 25%

Citadelle

Contrarian: The plan for this blend was to begin with a pure Oriental, then blend it with just enough Perique to neutralize the tongue bite, but no more. And no other ingredients. The balance point comes surprisingly close to the ratio of cows on the blend label. This blend lights and burns well. Nicotine is low-to-moderate. It still has a bit of a tang, but is much smoother than the pure Oriental. An Oriental version of Virginia / Perique blends. Contrarian is perfect for light, carefree, thought-free bowl of tobacco. It's perfect with a morning cup of coffee. To blend this with a different Oriental, start with a bowl of the pure Oriental. Note the acidity and bite. Then add Perique, starting with 6.25%, which is 1 part per 16. Smoke it. Increase the Perique only enough so the bite vanishes.

Contrarian
- Basma 81.25% (13 parts per 16)
- Perique 18.75% (3 parts per 16)

Basma Cavendish 31.25%
Burley Cavendish 37.5%
Burley 18.75%
Perique 6.25%
Basma 6.25%

Corridor: It's a day-long, muscle-liquefying hike from the South Rim of the Grand Canyon, down to the Colorado River. And the "corridor" is the easiest choice of route (complete with pavement and potties part of the way). It's also considered a "tourist" trail. Few real tourists (not backpackers) make it very far down, before proclaiming it to be a beautiful place, and promptly turning around to hightail it back to the rim. The corridor is both stunningly beautiful, and at the same time intimidating in its profligate geological revelations, as it snakes a hiker through two billion years of this planet's history.

This is a medium-body, all day smoke. It has no bite, but is a mouthful. I would have thought that, with all the burley, this blend does not need perique, but the little bit of perique rounds out the aroma profile, and smooths the blend. Surprisingly, I can't identify the Basma Cavendish or the Basma, or any of the other components in the taste and aroma. (Burley is present in the pouch aroma.) That distinctive burley aroma is somehow melded into the smoke. They all just cooperate. I would expect using an edgier Oriental (e.g. Bafra, Samsun, Trabzon, Shirazi) would lead to a different aroma mix--maybe better; maybe not, but definitely a bit more intense than the Basma blend.

If I were forced to guess the recipe from smoking a bowl of this, without seeing the actual tobacco or smelling the pouch, I could say for sure that there is no Virginia here, but the rest would be a puzzle. I don't even sense the perique as a recognizable aroma. Sensory conflation! If I were selling this blend commercially, I am certain that no competitor could come up with an approximation of the recipe.

The tiny proportion of Basma also offers a visual clue to the thoroughness of your mixing. If the scant Basma looks well distributed, then the similarly scant perique (which is not distinguishable by its color from all the other dark colors in the blend) is well distributed.

Corridor
- Basma Cavendish 31.25% (5 parts per 16)
- Burley Cavendish 37.50% (6 parts per 16)
- Burley Red Tip 18.75% (3 parts per 16)
- Basma 6.25% (1 part per 16)
- Perique 6.25% (1 part per 16)

Countryside: This 7 component blend presents a mild and measured pouch aroma. It is, in essence, a Virginia / Perique blend with a mere hint of Latakia, and a relatively gentle portion of a rich and slightly floral Oriental. The burn is excellent, and the nicotine is moderate. Despite 25% Perique, it does have a slight, Virginia tongue bite, so it should be smoked slowly. Although the slight bite will go away if you swap in one more part of Perique for one part of Double-Bright, doing that causes the overall blend to lose its mild character.

Countryside: an English Blend
- Flue-cured Virginia Lemon 6.25%
- Flue-cured Virginia Bright 6.25%
- Flue-cured Virginia Double-Bright 18.75%
- Flue-cured Virginia Red Cavendish 18.75%
- Basma 18.75%
- Latakia 6.25%
- Perique 25.00%

Cumbria: Including some of England's most breathtaking views, and its highest peaks, Lake District National Park, in the county of Cumbria, is a worldwide tourist destination. The dramatic valley shown in this blend label (looking toward the Irish Sea) was carved by the weight and movement of a massive glacier during the last Ice Age (which formed a transient "land" bridge between the British Isles and mainland Europe, and ended about 11,500 years ago).

This pipe blend is a medium-Latakia blend, moderate on the Virginia Bright, and a noticeable dose of burley. The Perique and Burley together smooth out the flue-cured bite. An excellent blend for mid-to-late in the day. Nicotine is medium.

Cumbria
- Latakia 37.5% (6 parts per 16)
- Burley 12.5% (2 parts per 16)
- Oriental 6.25% (1 part per 16)
- Virginia Bright 31.25% (5 parts per 16)
- Perique 12.5% (2 parts per 16)

Curiosity: A blend recipe by Steven Farmer (Fair Trade Tobacco Forum member, GreenDragon)

Curiosity:
- Burley 36%
- Virginia Red 23%
- Flue-cured (light) 23%
- Perique 18%

Notice that the Mars Curiosity rover on the blend label is navigating over the well-cured terrain of Martian tobacco leaf.

Debatable Lands: Along the westernmost border between Scotland and England there is a stretch of territory that was so lawless and considered so worthless that neither country would claim it, and be responsible for it. Clan fought clan, stealing back and forth from one another. Finally, when the two countries were joined under a single crown, authorities went in, hanged a bunch of clan leaders, and put an end to the debatable lands. The area is just north of Cumbria.

I would not consider this to be a "Latakia blend". It is an English-style blend. Or is it a Scottish-style blend? That's debatable. We'll call it a UK-style blend.

The tiny portion of Latakia subtly influences the pouch aroma, broadening it a bit. Instead, this is a feud between the Perique Clan and every other ingredient, since there is relatively little of bright (double-bright, at that) and Basma combined. The 50% lemon Cavendish surprisingly hovers in the background.

Nicotine is medium. Excellent burn. It does not leave a Latakia note in the air. The smoke tilts toward alkaline. I have smoked many bowls of this blend.

Debatable Lands
- Lemon Cavendish 50%
- Perique 20%
- Basma 14%
- Double-Bright 11%
- Latakia 5%

Delta Birdseye: With its square cross-section, perhaps Delta Goatseye might have been a better choice of a name for this pressed, whole-leaf blend. But then, once sliced, it looks more like a real bird's eye.

Three weeks of pressing renders the blend a bit fruitier and sweeter than unpressed. I smoke this by just breaking the flakes in half, then packing them into a pipe.

Burn is excellent. The pH balance is good. The general smoke aroma might be characterized as a balanced Virginia-Perique blend with a broader profile, and more robust nicotine content—coming in on the high side of medium.

I initially laid out the frog-legged leaf in rough proportions, then rolled them into a cigar. I used no glue, and no casing. This was pressed inside a narrow box for 3 weeks, using a clamp.

Delta Birdseye
- Virginia Bright 37.5%
- Basma 18.75%
- Perique 18.75%
- Dark Air-Cured Cavendish 12.5%
- Burley Red Tip 12.5%

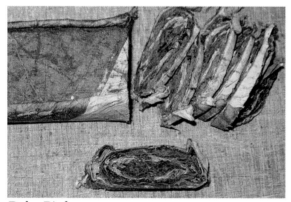

Delta Birdseye

Devil Eyed Frog: Unlike most of my pipe blends, I have made little effort in balancing the pH. The Devil Eye made me do it. The smoke leans firmly on the alkaline side of things. Aroma is about as full as I can handle. I think that any combination in the "little bit of this—a lot of that" level of precision will give you pretty much the same result.

Devil Eyed Frog
- VA Bright, kilned 25%
- Perique 20.8%
- One Sucker ligero Cavendish 18.75%
- Dark Air-Cured 10.4%
- Double Bright, kilned 8.33%
- Black Mammoth 8.33%
- Burley Red Tips 8.33%

Diamond Frog: Compared to my other "Frog" blends (Yellow Frog, Calico Frog, Black Frog and Top Frog), Diamond Frog is the mildest in taste and aroma. Its 25% Perique assures that the nicotine cruises just below medium, and the pH floats in a range that eliminates tongue bite from the Virginia and the Oriental. This will work well with other Oriental varieties. Expect Katerini, Bafra, Samsun and Trabzon to be somewhat more edgy, whereas any Basma type (Smyrna, Izmir, Xanthi, Yenidje, Prilep, etc.) will be similar to the stacked Basma. The same is true of other Virginia flue-cure variants, though the Perique proportion may require tweaking downward. Diamond Frog is also rather pretty to look at.

Diamond Frog
- WLT Stacked Basma 43.75%
- WLT Lemon Virginia 31.25%
- WLT Perique 25.00%

Diamond Frog

Dune Blend

Very dry, with a touch of Spice.

Dune Blend
- Basma 87.5%
- Perique 12.5%

Early Morning Smoke: This is a mild, floral blend, with a mild nicotine level. How floral it turns out to be will depend on which Oriental variety you've made into Cavendish. The same is also true of how smooth your blend turns out to be —depending on the initial acidity of the batch. I used my Trabzon Cavendish for my first blend. As with Orientals in the Samsun family (Bafra, Samsun, Katerini, Trabzon), the Trabzon Cavendish blend still had a soft edge. When I use WLT Basma (made into Cavendish) it required no more Perique to balance the tongue bite, and seems a little smoother than with the Trabzon. Most of the nicotine comes from the Perique.

Early Morning Smoke
- Oriental Cavendish 87.5% (14 parts of 16)
- Perique 12.5% (2 parts of 16)

Earth Rise: On the Moon, it might be the first thing in the morning, or late in the day, when Earth rises above your horizon. Either way, this straightforward blend (choice of tobacco varieties is limited, if you're living on the Moon) will fill your personal bubble dome with a rich aroma, and avoids the nasty, filter-clogging particulates that might come from burning Latakia. In blending with Cavendish at this ratio, the Perique is a little overstated, giving a slight tang at the back edges of my tongue.

As a Virginia / Perique blend, this has zero tongue bite, though surprisingly, the nicotine is medium-to-full. An enjoyable smoke. This seems to give a more intense nicotine hit than most of my other Virginia / Perique blends, I believe because of a higher pH.

[You may need to shave your head, and smoke this only while totally naked, so that when you rejoin your fellow Moon dwellers, you don't taint their carefully balanced fart and sweat atmosphere. Be considerate.]

Earth Rise
- Lemon Virginia Cavendish 62.5%
    (10 parts per 16)
- Perique 37.5%
    (6 parts per 16)

This is not a one-pony experience. **Exmoor** is a full-bodied blend with darker, deeper aromas and flavors dominating, despite over 50% flue-cured and Oriental combined. Nicotine is substantial. Burn is good. The relatively tiny proportion of burley (I used burley red tips) makes a noticeable difference in the character of the aroma.

With all varieties of tobacco, whether grown yourself or purchased, the strength, aroma and nicotine may vary from batch to batch, from growing season to growing season, and with how the leaf was ultimately finished and aged. I find this variability to be particularly significant with dark air-cured. So my "just right" blend for Exmoor may be different from your blend of the named ingredients. Since it teeters on the upper edge of reasonable strength for a pipe tobacco, you may find it to have gone over that edge.

If you wish to tone down its strength a bit, the finest increments can be made by reducing dark air-cured in exchange for Oriental. (I used stacked Basma for this blend.) Larger increments can be accomplished by reducing dark air-cured in exchange for flue-cured Virginia. (In my blending, I was using flue-cured Bright leaf.) A more aggressive approach to lowering the pH (decreasing nicotine absorption) would be to trade a bit of the perique for either Oriental or flue-cured. My quite coarse shred provides a slow and comfortable burn.

Exmoor
- Oriental 31.25% (5 parts per 16)
- Dark air-cured 25% (4 parts per 16)
- Flue-cured Virginia 25% (4 parts per 16)
- Perique 12.50% (2 parts per 16)
- Burley 6.25% (1 part per 16)

Exmoor (Omicron Variant)
- Krumovgrad T2 31.25% (5 parts per 16)
- Dark air-cured 25% (4 parts per 16)
- Flue-cured hand-tied Virginia 25% (4 parts per 16)
- Perique 9.375% (1½ parts per 16)
- Burley 9.375% (1½ parts per 16)

Exmoor #6 (another off-script delight)
- Katerini C2 31. parts per 16)
- 25% (5 parts per 16)
- One Sucker CAVENDISH 25% (4 parts per 16)
- Flue-cured "Double-Bright" Virginia 25% (4 parts per 16)
- Perique 6.25% (1 part per 16)
- Burley 12.5% (2 parts per 16)

Just changing the Katerini C2 (in Exmoor #6) to Katerini C4 makes Exmoor #7, and a noticeable difference. Part of the fun of pipe blending is to experiment with different varieties of a single, categorical ingredient, such as "Oriental". Sometimes, the impact of a subtle change, such as Krumovgrad T2 instead of Stacked Basma, can be surprising.

Forest Road: This blend began life as Greenbriar Two-Tone (50:50 Burley CAV and VA Bright CAV). But I wanted a little broader flavor profile, a rounder taste in the mouth, and to lower the smoke pH a tad. So this has a modest dose of both straight Burley Red Tip and straight VA Bright, along with sprinkle of Basma. The difference is quite noticeable. Although I am fond of very simple blends—simpler than this one, I am delighted with the result.

[I loved my beat up, two-tone (sky blue and white) Greenbriar van, when I was an impoverished student, back in 1968. Air-cooled, rear engine, automatic transmission, and enough space to do a side gig delivering 500 2-inch thick, city phone books to a large subdivision. The ignition lock assembly came right out of its socket, when I switched off the key, so I always left the key and its lock sitting in the dashboard ash tray. Nobody seemed interested in stealing my Greenbriar, even though this was St. Louis! But it had its limits. As does my Greenbriar Two-Tone pipe blend (see next page).]

The pouch aroma is inviting and complex. I find it interesting how such tiny amounts of straight Burley Red Tip and VA Bright influence the strength and mood of this mostly Cavendish blend. This all day smoke comes in at medium-to-full nicotine.

Forest Road
- Burley Red Tip Cavendish 41.7% (~6½ parts per 16)
- Virginia Bright Cavendish 41.7% (~6½ parts per 16)
- Burley Red Tip 4.1% (~¾ part per 16)
- Virginia Bright 4.1% (~¾ part per 16)
- Basma 8.4% (~1½ parts per 16)

Gentle On My Mine: Warm, soft and slightly sweet. No tongue bite. Medium-to-full nicotine. This is the blend I entered for the forum's Imagination Challenge. I've simply given it a label of mine.

[WARNING: The State of California has determined that this blend has not been adequately tested for safety in the presence of a canary.]

Gentle on my Mine
- PA Maduro Cavendish 18.75% (3 parts per 16)
- Maryland Cavendish 18.75% (3 parts per 16)
- VA Red Flue-cured 62.50% (10 parts per 16)

Photo by Brian Gratwicke

Golden Frog: Katerini is an Oriental in the same family as Samsun, Bafra and Trabzon. I find it more peppery than Basma type Orientals. Little Yellow is a unique dark air-cured variety that cures to an orange-brown, is a bit lower in nicotine than most other dark air-cured leaf varieties, but provides a rounder, more aromatic character. The smoke of Little Yellow is a little less alkaline than other dark air-cured, which makes a difference in balancing it with either flue-cured or Oriental leaf.

This particular blend leans toward the acidic side, which can cause some tongue bite, if you smoke it too rapidly. The aroma is mild and well rounded. Nicotine level seems medium. I find this enjoyable early in the day.

Golden Frog
- Katerini 62.5%
- Little Yellow 37.5%

Golden-ish Frog
- Oriental 62.5%
- Dark Air-Cured 37.5%

Greenbrier Two-Tone: Sorry. No seat belts. This simple, all Cavendish blend is as smooth as can be. But the burley red tip still has all its nicotine, despite the Cavendish process. It sneaks up on you without warning. But don't worry. The engine is an air-cooled, opposing 6 cylinder, with tons of horsepower and practically zero vibration. (And gas is only 31 cents a gallon, and cigarettes are 26 cents a pack!)

In reality, the blend is a nearly homogeneous, medium brown color. But its aroma profile is more complex than its blend name might suggest. This is a kinder, gentler and non-adulterated take on the "drug store" blend called Half and Half [from Lane Ltd.], which is half burley and half bright leaf, is fairly harsh stuff, and heavily cased.

Greenbrier Two-Tone
- Virginia Bright Cavendish 50%
- Burley Red Cavendish 50%

High Desert Frog: This is a simple blend. It is rich, relatively smooth, and with a barely detectable tongue bite from the Krumovgrad. Nicotine is moderate. I don't notice any "cigar" aroma coming from the Peru ligero Cavendish. Burn is fairly good, and it tends to generate clouds of smoke. Krumovgrad initially dominates the pouch aroma, but this subsides after several days of resting the blend.

This recipe is a reasonable place to start. Depending on your batch of leaf, specific tobacco varieties and extent of Cavendish cooking, you can wiggle the proportions, to find a happy pH balance.

High Desert Frog
- Krumovgrad 68.75%
- Peru Ligero Cavendish 31.25%

Desert Amphibian
- Basma or other Oriental 68.75%
- Upper leaf cigar Cavendish 31.25%

Photo: Bjørnar G. Hansen

Hubble Bubble
- Little Yellow Cavendish 25%
- Basma 75%

Hubble Bubble: No. No. No. It's not about galaxy-ripping quasar tsunamis in space. But Hubble bubble is an astronomical concept. The Hubble constant is a measurement of how fast the universe is expanding. Everything in the universe constantly expands—including the cigars in your humidor (along with the humidor and your cigar cutter, of course). A Hubble bubble is a localized region where the Hubble constant hiccups.

This galaxy-ripping pipe blend tsunami makes a great bowl of tobacco for late in the day. As an alternative, you can make it with any dark air-cured Cavendish and any Oriental.

Jaipur: The pouch aroma of this blend is dominated by the floral Krumovgrad, a Basma-type tobacco grown in the Rhodope Mountains of Bulgaria, not too far from Xanthi Greece. I can't really say if the difference between Krumovgrad and Basma is the variety itself, or the sun-curing methods. But they are different.

My supply of India Dark Air-Cured tobacco seems smoother than the American Dark Air-Cured that I have played with, but this may be due to age. The India Dark Air is from a 2011 crop. It's nicotine is full, and is alkaline enough to balance all the Virginia and Krumovgrad nicely. I suspect (only a suspicion) that the room note of this blend is similar to that of the back streets of Jaipur.

There is an edginess to the taste. Aroma is rich and distinctly different. Burn is excellent, and the nicotine of the blend is medium-to-full. This is not a timid blend.

If you have no access to India Dark Air-Cured, then it's your turn to change the Jaipur.

Jaipur
- India Dark Air-Cured 31.25% (5 parts per 16)
- Lemon Virginia 37.5% (6 parts per 16)
- Krumovgrad 31.25% (5 parts per 16)

Just Walking Home: I made this blend with fire-cured Shirazi. If you use Kentucky fire-cured, you may need to significantly reduce the proportion of fire-cured in the blend, since its nicotine will be much higher. Pouch aroma is subdued, slightly fruity (from the Perique), and offers just a hint of the fire-cured. The blend lights easily, and burns well. Nicotine is mild to medium.

Just Walking Home
- Fire-cured Oriental 31.25%
- Virginia Double Bright 31.25%
- Burley Red Tip Cavendish 18.75%
- Perique 12.5%
- Basma 6.25%

Karpas is the distinctive, long peninsula that juts out from the northeast of the Island of Cyprus. Most, if not all tobacco that has been grown in Cyprus has been grown in what has become the "Turkish", northern Cyprus.

The aroma of the Cyprus Oriental is clearly a "Turkish" aroma. Alone, it is quite spicy, and bites the tongue. To balance it, I've used India Dark Air-cured, which is more potent than American Dark Air varieties. The Burley Red Tip brings the pH into a happy zone, and broadens the aroma. Burn is excellent. Aroma is full. Nicotine is medium-to-full. The room note is "robust" enough that even I noticed it.

Karpas

- Cyprus Oriental mw 62.5%
- India Dark Air-cured 25.0%
- Burley Red Tip 12.5%

Lake Bled
- Prilep 37.50%
- Burley Red Tip Cavendish 25.00%
- Virginia Red 18.75%
- Perique 12.50%
- Dark Air Cured 6.25%

NINETY MORE PIPE BLENDS

Lake Shkodra, the largest lake in Southern Europe, lies on the border between Albania and Montenegro. Most of the tobacco grown in Albania has long been the Oriental varieties, like Xanthi, Bafra and a number of others. As in many other countries, the tobacco growers of Albania are turning more and more away from tobacco and to other crops, such as herbs, to pay their bills. For a long time, they had been required to sell their tobacco to a foreign-based monopoly, at whatever price the monopoly would offer. Today, that has changed. Domestic buyers are now permitted, and the foreign monopoly is paying higher tariffs. So perhaps tobacco growers will grow more tobacco in Albania once again.

This blend is low in nicotine, mild and lightly floral in aroma. The slight edge of tongue bite common with pure Orientals is softened by the tiny portion of Dark Air. Replacing 6.35% of the Basma (that's 1 part per 16) with an equivalent amount of additional Dark Air makes a significant difference in the taste, aroma and nicotine, and might be worth your experimentation.

Lake Shkodra
- Basma 50% (8 parts per 16)
- Samsun 43.75% (7 parts per 16)
- Dark Air-Cured 6.25% (1 part per 16)

Long Red CAVEndish: Surprisingly full pouch aroma. Burns well. Unlike Cavendish that I've made of other cigar varieties, this doesn't smell at all like "cigar". Nicotine is medium. The smoke aroma is rich and enjoyable. No tongue bite. I suspect that PA Red Cavendish, Little Dutch Cavendish and Dutch (Ohio) Cavendish might also work for this, since all four seem to be in the same general flavor family. But I haven't yet made those other three into Cavendish. A reasonable substitute might be a Pennsylvania seedleaf or broadleaf variety.

Long Red CAVEndish blend
- Long Red Cavendish 50% (8 parts per 16)
- VA Bright 37.5% (6 parts per 16)
- Perique 12.5% (2 parts per 16)

Krumovgrad 81.25%
Dark Air-Cured 18.75%

Marudnik

Marudnik is a superb blend for your first pipe of the day. In the Rhodope mountain range of southern Bulgaria, the source of the Krumovgrad tobacco variety, Marudnik (a pancake topped with yogurt or fruit) is more of a dessert than an appetizer.

Krumovgrad is a Basma-type Oriental tobacco. It's pouch aroma is quite floral, while the acidity of its smoke is not as pronounced as that of Basma, Yenidje or Xanthi. Like these latter three varieties, the burn of Krumovgrad is adequate, though not great. It's nicotine content is quite low. In this blend, I used Dark Air-Cured to balance the acidity and crank up the nicotine, while broadening the darker aspects of the aroma.

Марудник (Marudnik)
- Krumovgrad 81.25% (13 parts per 16)
- Dark Air-Cured 18.75% (3 parts per 16)

Monarch: A soft, mild smoke. Monarch offers a slight edge to the taste. The tiny amount of straight Burley provides a fullness that is lacking in the Cavendish version of burley. I would rate the nicotine as a solid medium.

The downside of this blend is that Burley is rather hygroscopic (water attracting), and when Cavendish processed is even more hygroscopic. So it has a tendency to swell a bit at the bottom of the bowl, requiring delicate work with the tamper. Basma, of all the Orientals, seldom burns particularly well. The combination of all the Burley Cavendish and the Basma means that you should smoke these in a drier than usual state.

Monarch
- Burley Red Tip Cavendish 50%
- Burley Red Tip 6.25%
- Basma 43.75%

Photo: Flickr/usfwmidwest

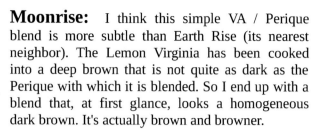

Moonrise: I think this simple VA / Perique blend is more subtle than Earth Rise (its nearest neighbor). The Lemon Virginia has been cooked into a deep brown that is not quite as dark as the Perique with which it is blended. So I end up with a blend that, at first glance, looks a homogeneous dark brown. It's actually brown and browner.

Moonrise is an anytime smoke--a mild enough aroma for a first pipe, and rich enough in nicotine for late evening. I made the Lemon VA Cavendish from WLT Lemon VA, and the Perique is WLT Perique. So if you go with your own take on Cavendish and Perique, you may have to do some tinkering with my 3:1 ratio.

Moonrise
- Lemon Virginia Cavendish 75%
- Perique 25%

BONUS BLEND

Moonscape: There is no recipe! It uses two varieties of Cavendish. The first is fairly straightforward: Flue-cured Virginia Red Cavendish. The second is a Cavendish made of random short scraps from cigar rolling.

I used VA Red Cavendish for both a wrapper and a binder, then rolled a cigar using entirely cigar short scrap Cavendish as the filler. The diameter of the cigar that you roll will determine the ratio between the two ingredients. It is rolled into a cigar to facilitate slicing an even shred.

Moonscape
- Flue-cured Virginia Red Cavendish
- Random Cigar short scrap Cavendish

Photo: Ollie Taylor

Noctilucent Knowlton is serious. Don't be fooled by the noctilucence. It's nicotine is about as full as you will ever find in one of my pipe blends.

The pouch aroma of Noctilucent Knowlton is mild and fragrant, perhaps even floral. Cavendish processing can sometimes bring that out—without added flavorants. Room note is...well...I assume fairly intense, though I couldn't smell anything for 30 minutes after smoking a bowl. Smoke aroma is enjoyable. Burn is moderate, since it is all Cavendish.

As for making this blend, you will have to cook each of the varieties into Cavendish yourself. The Little Yellow, Long Red, Black Mammoth and Silver River are usually not commercially available.

The moral of this blend (Yes, even pipe blends can have a moral.) is that you can mix and match all varieties of Cavendish only, and come up with your own, interesting pipe blends. The greater the number of distinct aromas and flavors, the less any one of them will be easily identifiable. And certain (usually surprise) combinations of multiple aromas seem to trick our olfactory senses into "recognizing" something entirely new and different from the components of the blend.

The nicotine strength of the original tobacco will determine its nicotine strength when made into Cavendish.

Noctilucent Knowlton
- Virginia Red Flue-Cured Cavendish 18.75% (3 of 16 parts)
- Little Yellow Cavendish 18.75% (3 of 16 parts)
- Dark Air-Cured Cavendish 12.5% (2 of 16 parts)
- Long Red Cavendish 12.5% (2 of 16 parts)
- Black Mammoth Cavendish 12.5% (2 of 16 parts)
- Pennsylvania Ligero Cavendish 12.5% (2 of 16 parts)
- Silver River Cavendish 12.5% (2 of 16 parts)

Old Guy: This simple blend offers a tasty Virginia/perique, subdued by a generous proportion of Basma. Medium nicotine. There is a slight edge. As with all VA/Per blends, the blend itself needs to rest a few days after blending, in order to meld the perique into the pouch aroma (so it smells yummy and intriguing, instead of barnyard stinky). This blend is enjoyable and relatively mild, though robust enough for an all day smoke. Nothing challenging or "educational" or exploratory here. It just cruises along in the background of your day.

A smooth, mild Oriental can tame a more potent blend, without dramatically altering its general aroma.

Old Guy's Blend
- Basma 56.25%
- Virginia Bright Cavendish 25.00%
- Perique 18.75%

Pearl of Shibam was my very first pipe blend, and my very first blend label. It is a typical English-Latakia pipe blend, with modest Latakia. I have not altered the blend, but felt that its label ought to reflect the label style of all of my other blend labels. *(Again, the Arabic says, "al sharq", which means "The East")*

Pearl of Shibam
- Flue-cured Virginia 31.25% (5 parts per 16)
- Oriental 25% (4 parts per 16)
- Latakia 25% (4 parts per 16)
- Perique 18.75% (3 parts per 16)

Perk Up
- Flue-cured Virginia Red Cavendish 2/3
- Beerique 1/3

Peruvian Frog: Peruvian ligero cigar leaf is "drier" and less aromatic than Caribbean and Central American cigar leaf. But it's nicotine strength is similar to most other varieties of ligero. Making it into Cavendish noticeably smooths its edges, and seems to add a vague, floral quality. Of course, the Cavendish process does not alter its nicotine content. (I tried a small bowl of pure Peruvian ligero Cavendish, and had to space it out over several hours to finish it, despite its wonderful aroma.)

Pouch aroma is softer and gentler than the smoke aroma. The proportions in this blend seem to balance the acidity of the Lemon Virginia Cavendish and the Basma. So there is no tongue bite here. The nicotine of the blend is medium-to-full. I don't detect any distinctive "cigar" character to the blend. The Basma lends a subtle crispness. For a blend that is ¾ Cavendish, the burn is surprisingly good. I'll leave the room note for you to evaluate.

Peruvian Frog
- Peru Ligero Cavendish 37.5% (6 parts per 16)
- Lemon Virginia Cavendish 37.5% (6 parts per 16)
- Basma 25% (4 parts per 16)

BONUS BLEND *with* BEERIQUE

Perk Up: Beerique is a Perique curing process developed by Steven Farmer (FTT forum member, GreenDragon), and is discussed in its own chapter of this book. Essentially, it uses a variety of brewers yeast, instead of depending on the traditional, *Pichia anomala* yeast to alter the tobacco. While flue-cured Virginia Red (upper leaf) is less acidic when made into Cavendish, it's nicotine level is considerably higher than flue-cured Virginia from lower on the stalk (e.g. Virginia Bright). The blend here (with exact proportions depending on both your choice of Beerique leaf variety and the priming level of the Cavendish) is aimed at eliminating the tongue bite of the pure Cavendish.

This is smooth and potent, with the dark richness of the VA Red Cavendish, merged with a light fruitiness of the Beerique. It burns well, and presents a medium-to-full nicotine.

Photo: FL International Univ., Germán Chávez

Playful Mammoth: Envision yourself on a beautiful, sunny day, during a much needed pause in the tedium of everyday life, being playfully lifted into the air on the curvy, smooth tusk of a playful mammoth. The Savannah has deep grass, so you probably won't actually break a bone. It's just a game. You hold up a weapon, and throw it. Then the playful mammoth happily runs to fetch you.

Although this blend has a substantial proportion of Latakia, which makes it rich and smoky, the 25% Black Mammoth Cavendish is really in the driver's seat. It is that Black Mammoth CAV giving the blend its full nicotine, and without Perique. There is not much here that requires pH balancing. The Basma is mostly cosmetic—part of its visual presentation.

Dark, rich, smoky and full. A satisfying blend for late in the day. (Room note is way better than that of a mammoth.) Even though Black Mammoth is a Dark Air-cured variety, it has its own distinctive taste. Lacking flue-cured leaf in the blend, it goes fairly well after smoking a cigar.

Playful Mammoth
- Black Mammoth Cavendish 25% (4 parts per 16)
- Latakia 62.5 % (10 parts per 16)
- Basma 12.5% (2 parts per 16)

Ptarmigan Hiding: This blend is deep and rich. If you manage to spot this Ptarmigan Hiding in plain sight, and fire it up, it raises a ruckus. The Dark-Air Cavendish is softer than uncooked Dark-Air, but is still intense. So despite the proportions of each of the ingredients, the Dark-Air Cavendish dominates—full and satisfying. There is no tongue bite. Nicotine is medium-full.

Ptarmigan Hiding
- Oriental 25.00% (4 parts per 16)
- Virginia Bright 32.25% (5 parts per 16)
- Dark-Air Cavendish 25.00% (4 parts per 16)
- Perique 18.75% (3 parts per 16)

Ptarmigan Summer

- Oriental 25%
- flue cured 10%
- Dark air 5%
- Burley 32.5%
- flue-cured Cavendish 27.5%

A medium, balanced burley blend.

Punta Ventana 2020: In early January of 2020, a rare, natural arch window along Puerto Rico's southern coast was destroyed by a 5.8 magnitude earthquake. Punta Ventana has been a well known tourist attraction for over a century. The natural wonder is now gone. Arch windows within a jutting finger of sedimentary layers are relatively rare at any given point in time. But the windows are a common part of the progression of erosion to a sedimentary rock peninsula. So on a geologic time scale, their occurrence is common, and their existence always transient. On a human time scale, their destruction seems more surprising. Another earthquake (5.5 magnitude) struck near the same area May 2, 2020.

This blend is my gesture of acknowledgment to Puerto Rico for their lost treasure. It is a mid-day blend, with medium nicotine, a full aroma, and no tongue bite. My testing blends used WLT Basma Cavendish and burley red tip Cavendish. The Perique is from WLT. With the high proportion of Oriental Cavendish, a bowl of Punta Ventana doesn't last very long, so a pipe with a large bowl is in order.

Punta Ventana 2020
- Oriental Cavendish 75.0%
- Burley Cavendish 12.5%
- Perique 12.5%

Raggedy Owl
- Virginia Red Flue-cured 31.25% (5 parts per 16)
- Black Mammoth Cavendish 25% (4 parts per 16)
- Perique 18.75% (3 parts per 16)
- Düzce 18.75% (3 parts per 16)
- Dark Air-cured 6.25% (1 part per 16)

Raggedy Fowl
- Virginia Flue-cured 31.25% (5 parts per 16)
- Dark Air-cured Cavendish 25% (4 parts per 16)
- Perique 18.75% (3 parts per 16)
- Oriental 18.75% (3 parts per 16)
- Dark Air-cured 6.25% (1 part per 16)

Red Admiral: A soft, mild smoke. The tiny amount of straight Burley provides a fullness that is lacking in the Cavendish version of burley. I would rate the nicotine as a solid medium.

Red Admiral
Burley Red Tip Cavendish 56.25% (9 parts per 16)
Burley Red Tip 6.25% (1 part per 16)
Basma 37.5% (6 parts per 16)

Raggedy Owl is a mild-to-medium strength blend. The Virginia Red provides a soft background to the taste and aroma, while the Black Mammoth Cavendish rumbles out the bass notes. The pH is balanced with the Perique and a smidgen of Dark Air-cured, so there is no tongue bite. My Düzce (a Turkish Basma type) is softer and smoother than most other Basmas. This can be considered a mild, all-day smoke. It's pouch aroma is gentle and inviting. I can barely detect the aroma of the Perique.

My coarse shred contributes to a gradual and steady burn. The name, Raggedy Owl, is probably more descriptive of how I was feeling, prior to enjoying a bowl of it. There is nothing raggedy about the aroma.

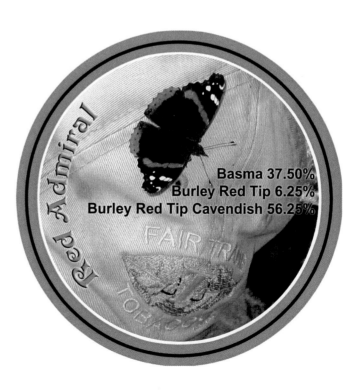

Virginia Red 25%   Burley Red 12.5%
Virginia Red Cavendish 25%
Burley Red Cavendish 25%
Long Red 12.5%

Red Caboose AND Red Train

During the late 1920s and into the 1940s, many old, decommissioned railroad passenger cars were planted in cities and along highways, and converted into restaurants, known as "diners", after the dining cars of the railroads. By the 1940s these were often no longer old rail cars, but prefabricated for delivery on site, like a mobile home. So even these later diners looked like rail cars. (Perhaps all those squeaky train wheels encouraged diners to always serve greasy food—so troublesome to adequately wash off the spoons.) Today, real diners have pretty much been displaced by fast-food franchises, though some restaurant chains still cling to the diner motif (e.g. Waffle House).

Cabooses (the sight of which was my sole motivation for patiently watching every long, slow freight train when I was a child in the 1950s) have mostly vanished from the rails, but still show up occasionally as diners or as mini-motels, or even as a backyard man cave. Unlike the real diners of yesteryear, converted cabooses today charge boutique prices for their kale and tofu.

The Red Train blend consists of red, red, red, and red. It is half Cavendish. Red Caboose is similar, also with half Cavendish, but with a nice measure of cigar leaf tagged onto the end, displacing some of the Virginia Red.

Virginia Red Cavendish 25%
Virginia Red 37.5%   Burley Red 12.5%
Burley Red Cavendish 25%

Red Caboose
- Virginia Red Cavendish 25%
  (4 parts per 16)
- Burley Red Tips Cavendish 25%
  (4 parts per 16)
- Virginia Red 25% (4 parts per 16)
- Burley Red Tips 12.5% (2 parts per 16)
- Long Red (or Pennsylvania Red) 12.5%
  (2 parts per 16)

Red Train
- Virginia Red Cavendish 25%
  (4 parts per 16)
- Burley Red Tips Cavendish 25%
  (4 parts per 16)
- Virginia Red 37.5% (6 parts per 16)
- Burley Red Tips 12.5% (2 parts per 16)

Reflection: This smooth, bite-free blend features a mild-to-medium nicotine level, a broad aroma profile, and a sweet, complex pouch aroma. (No smokiness or stinkies here.) My own tests used an Oriental mixture, with roughly half of it WLT Stacked Basma and the rest aged, sun-cured and kilned Cyprus "Samsun". The Burley Red Tip has been kilned.

Reflection
- Oriental 70%
- VA Red Flue-cured 12.5%
- Burley Red Tips 12.5%
- Dark Air-cured 5%

Sailing to Trabzon: I used home-grown Trabzon made into Latakia. It had been sun-cured prior to firing. Seven weeks of firing, subsequent kilning for 8 weeks, followed by about 1 month of rest significantly reduced the raw "fire-cured" aroma. But it still had a noticeable, subtle campfire aroma.

Since there is no point in smoking any Latakia straight—it's always just too potent, I decided to give it a try in a blend already known to me, and one that I enjoy. For the basis of this blend, I used my recipe for Pearl of Shibam, substituting home-fired Latakia for the usual Cyprus Latakia. It was initially not to my liking. After the shredded blend rested as a blend for about 1 week, the campfire aroma receded further, and ultimately offered a Latakia pouch aroma of incense. My expectation is that the aroma merging that occurs within a blend will continue to improve this with more time.

Sailing to Trabzon
- Home-fired Latakia 25% (~4 parts per 16)
- Lemon Virginia 31% (~5 parts per 16)
- Perique 19% (~3 parts per 16)
- Basma 25% (~4 parts per 16)

Shades of Dark: For those of you who prefer a deep, full-flavored blend, without the pungency of Perique or the smokiness of Latakia, Shades of Dark blends 3 Cavendish varieties. The nicotine is near the upper end of medium-to-full bodied. Unlike Caribbean cigar varieties, PA Maduro—especially as a Cavendish—does not permeate the room with a cigar-like aroma. Despite the Dark Air and PA Maduro proportions, there is still a slight tongue bite with this. That could be remedied with one more part of Dark Air Cavendish (6.25%) replacing one part of VA Bright Cavendish, but that significantly jacks up the nicotine hit. Another approach would be to replace some of the Bright Cavendish with an Oriental Cavendish.

Shades of Dark
- Virginia Bright Cavendish 62.5% (10 parts per 16)
- Pennsylvania Maduro Cavendish 18.75% (3 parts per 16)
- Dark Air-Cured Cavendish 18.75% (3 parts per 16)

Shinumo was an attempt to utilize unflavored, commercial "black" Cavendish. Despite having no flavored casing added, it remained squishy and "black", only because of a heavy dose of propylene glycol (PG), added at the factory. I spread it in a tray, and heated it to about 140°F for many hours, to drive off as much of the PG as I could. The PG could still be detected afterwards, and, unlike pure leaf, the shred never fully dried.

This blend is a presentable smoke, though my mouth easily felt the presence of the residual PG (like you get with any "drug store" pouch of commercial tobacco).

Shinumo
- MD 609 Cavendish 31.25%
- Stoved Commercial Cavendish 68.75%

Silver Lining: This is another of my attempts to make a smokable blend of Silver River Cavendish. My problem is that Silver River contains some sort of terpene that I find unpleasant. It's still there in the Cavendish. So I decided to use a blunt instrument with this one. It contains fully 25% Silver River Cavendish. The Silver River Cavendish leaves a bit of a "cigar" room note, and I continue to be suspicious that it is a renamed version of Bolivia Criollo Black, or a related Bolivian or Paraguayan variety, like Flojo.

[Names of tobacco varieties are often uninformative, sometimes misleading. "Moonlight" and "Magnolia" sound truly charming, but are simply a slight variation of Connecticut Shade. Silver River was a name assigned by a US hobby grower who thought it had something of a natural menthol to it—it does not. But he had lost track of its actual varietal name. So we now have the charming name, "Silver River".]

Back to this blend. Somehow, the robust dose of Silver River Cavendish, with a similar quantity of Burley Red Tip Cavendish, together balance the pH of the Lemon Virginia Cavendish. What I found surprising is that the combination seems to play happy games together. That is, I don't taste the icky terpene that I know is still there. Somehow, the other blend components mask its taste.

The science of odorant perception:
- production
- release
- detection
- identification

A) The terpene is already in the tobacco
B) we know it is released with combustion
C) we know we must be smelling/tasting it; but...
D) another odorant within the combusting tobacco tricks our senses into not identifying the presence of this terpene. Yay!

Similarly, I don't taste the usually distinctive note of Burley Red Tip Cavendish. Its nicotine is on the high side. Although I might regret being stranded on a desert island with only this particular blend to smoke, those who have a supply of Silver River may want to give this a try.

Silver Lining
- Lemon Virginia Cavendish 50%
- Burley Cavendish 25%
- Silver River Cavendish 25%

Skree: A non-pressed version of Talus Flake. Specific to the Talus Flake blend, smoking a pipe with broken flakes jammed into the bowl is curious. With only two components, acidic Virginia lemon and relatively alkaline Perique in the Talus Flake, I can actually sense a shifting tongue sensation, between the front and back, as the bowl is smoked.

The pressing of Talus Flake does enhance a slight fruitiness in the aroma. The burn is spectacular. I find it smooth, interesting and enjoyable. The whole pressing thing is a bit of a bother, since the same recipe using unpressed shred is similar. But I do detect a difference between the two. I guess I could call the unpressed-shredded blend Skree.

For those too pressed for time to press their Talus Flake tobacco blend:

Smaug

Skree
- flue-cured Lemon Virginia 62.5% (10 parts per 16)
- Perique 37.5% (6 parts per 16)

Smaug: Very smokey, but you must provide your own fire. It's not about the Tolkien character. Smaug is actually this creature's genus. How suggestive! The blend is not for the timid. The Oriental (I used Basma) is mostly for looks, though I can taste it in there somewhere. Latakia alone doesn't provide much nicotine, given its intensity of taste and aroma, since it is made from a Basma-type leaf. So the Dark Air is to crank it up a bit. Plan this for your final pipe of the day. I have to say that I really like this blend. Two bowls of this in a row will make your tongue feel like a doormat.

Smaug
- Latakia 75%
- Oriental 18.75%
- Dark Air-Cured 6.25%

Screen capture from https://earth.nullschool.net/

Smoky Man: Although this is indeed smoky, from its hefty proportion of Latakia, it is a surprisingly smooth smoke. The Dark Air-Cured Cavendish perfectly balances the acidity of the Basma, while not really cranking up the nicotine as much as I would expect, especially when compared to burley. Nicotine is medium. The aroma spectrum is understandably narrow, though the pouch aroma is engaging. It makes a wonderful pipeful for later in the day, and is not so heavy as to limit it to your last pipe for the day.

The image of Smoky Man on the blend label is actually a real thing. It's from a real-time atmospheric map of particulates in the Pacific Ocean, just west of the California coast, one late summer afternoon during the record breaking fire season of 2020. I have not modified it. (You can spot a vertical, longitude grid line passing through his left eye.)

Any oriental can be used, and the Dark Air-Cured Cavendish might be reasonably replaced with burley Cavendish.

Smoky Man
- Latakia 62.5% (10 parts per 16)
- Basma 25% (4 parts per 16)
- Dark Air-Cured Cavendish 12.5% (2 parts per 16)

Sultan Qaboos: Fashioned in the tradition of my Red Caboose pipe blend, this one honors the late Sultan of Oman, Sultan Qaboos bin Said Al Said, known for his quiet diplomacy during his five decade reign. This blend offers mild to medium nicotine, and not a trace of sweetness—only desert dryness. With 87.5% Cavendish, one can imagine the steamy waters of the Gulf.

Sultan Qaboos
- Samsun 12.50% (2 parts per 16)
- Trabzon Cavendish 18.75% (3 parts per 16)
- VA Red Cavendish 31.25% (5 parts per 16)
- Burley Red Cavendish 31.25%
     (5 parts per 16)
- Dark Air Cavendish 6.25% (1 part per 16)

If you don't have Samsun and/or Trabzon Cavendish, then definitely give it a try with whichever Oriental(s) you may have.

Sunday Afternoon: Sunday dinner is over. Kick back with your favorite pipe and an uncomplicated, relaxing blend that demands nothing. No analysis. No revelations or delicate interplay of contrasting components.

This burley / Virginia pipe blend uses simple ingredients in a simple 5:3 ratio. It may look like a typical, cigarette blend, but by using Burley Red Tips, rather than the more common, lower leaf, the body is richer and the flavor profile more complex. I've left it with a slight flue-cured edge.

Sunday Afternoon
- Virginia Bright 62.5% (10 parts per 16)
- Burley Red Tip 37.5% (6 parts per 16)

Sunset: This blend is for late in the day. It is rich and full, with a generous nicotine hit. The most distinctive aroma is that of Little Yellow Cavendish. While you can and should make Cavendish from other dark air-cured varieties, Little Yellow is unique among them. Its color, flavor and the character of its aroma are different from the others, when simply air-cured. It's nicotine is a peg lower as well. But that means you can command more of its aroma in your blend, without laying you flat. In its Cavendish incarnation, the edges are softer and smoother, but the unique aroma and nicotine persist.

As usual, I use a relatively wide shred (hand-shredded), since I prefer its slower burn. Because of this blend's simplicity, it is a great starting point, with likely adjustments easiest between the Little Yellow Cavendish quantity and the Flue-cured Virginia quantity.

A curious attribute of blends with a significant proportion of dark air-cured is that the pH of the smoke is in the same range as that of cigar smoke. So if you are inclined to switch between pipe and cigar during the same day, there is not the unpleasant taste transition attributable to what I will call pH shock. No cigar taste or aroma, but it plays nicely when your mouth and tongue have recently enjoyed a cigar.

Sunset
- Flue-cured Virginia Bright 37.5% (6 parts per 16)
- Little Yellow Cavendish 37.5% (6 parts per 16)
- Flue-cured Virginia Bright Cavendish 25% (4 parts per 16)

Sunspot: That small bit of Little Yellow Cavendish (a mere 6.25%) is enough to lend Little Yellow's characteristically warm, full and quite unique aroma to this morning-through-night pipe blend.   That seems surprising, in comparison to the Cavendish I've made from other Dark Air-Cured tobacco varieties.   And with the Virginia Bright cooked into a Cavendish, the 18.75% One Sucker (burley) Cavendish balances the pH, eliminating tongue bite. Burn is excellent. Nicotine is medium.

Sunspot
- Virginia Bright Cavendish 75.00%
- One Sucker Cavendish 18.75%
- Little Yellow Cavendish 6.25%

Sunsmudge
- Virginia Cavendish 75.00%
- Any Dark Air-Cured Cavendish 25%

Super Blood Wolf Moon Eclipse: This was a bonus blend in my previous pipe-blending book. The recipe is unchanged, but this new label is more evocative. Astronomical events need to be spiced up a bit for mass media consumption. So we have been fed, "Super Blood Wolf Moon Eclipse".

The strength is a mild-to-medium. Perhaps I should shorten the blend name to just "Blood Moon", but that's not as much fun.

Super Blood Wolf Moon Eclipse
- Flue-cured Virginia Red 25%
- Flue-cured Virginia Red Cavendish 18.75%
- Kilned Burley Red Tips 25%
- Kilned Burley Red Tips Cavendish 18.75%
- Latakia 12.5%

Takin A Break: The Himalayan takin is in the same sub-family as sheep and goats (though closer to sheep than goats). But, unlike most familiar caprines, the takin can exceed 850 pounds.

Don't let its golden fleece trick you into thinking this pipe blend is a cuddly pushover. The Katerini provides a vibrancy, but all the muscle lies in the other three components. It's a smooth smoke, with medium to full nicotine. I suspect that you will be surprised at how a mere 9.38% Perique influences the pouch aroma as well as the tongue feel and pH. Little Yellow and Long Red, both cooked into Cavendish, might be considered hefty ingredients riding on touring-grade shock absorbers.

Little Yellow is a dark air-cured variety, though a shaver milder and more flavorful than most. Long Red is in the same grouping as Little Dutch, Dutch Ohio and Pennsylvania Red, though any broadleaf or seedleaf cigar type would do as a substitute. Katerini is a petiolate Oriental, in the same family as Samsun, Bafra and Trabzon. In a pinch, any other Oriental can serve here. With alternative ingredients, I would suggest leaving the Perique the same, and adjusting the dark air-cured to the Oriental, in order to balance the pH. (That pH balance is what determines tongue bite or lack thereof. I don't use a pH meter; just my tongue. Tip bite: lower the Oriental. Back-tongue bite: increase the Oriental.)

Takin A Break
- Little Yellow Cavendish 37.50% (6 parts per 16)
- Long Red Cavendish 31.25% (5 parts per 16)
- Katerini C2 21.87% (3½ parts per 16)
- Perique 9.38% (1½ parts per 16)

Takin A Break Sheepishly
- Dark Air-Cured Cavendish 37.50% (6 parts per 16)
- Cigar leaf Cavendish 31.25% (5 parts per 16)
- Oriental 21.87% (3½ parts per 16)
- Perique 9.38% (1½ parts per 16)

Talus Flake: When a rocky peak or cliff weathers, large and small rocks are created. They eventually fall down the cliff, and settle into a steep slope of relatively loose rocks. This is sometimes called a scree slope, sometimes a talus slope. (Scree is gravel size, whereas talus is generally described as larger rocks—fist-size to washing machine size.)

Well, I've taken to hyperbole in naming this blend. It is essentially a blend of flue-cured Virginia and Perique that his been rolled into a "cigar", pressed into a plug, then sliced into flake. (Talus!) [The method and result are illustrated on pages 16-17.]

One might argue that this is actually sliced twist (sometimes called "rounds"), but it is more specifically a sliced, pressed VaPer cigar (rounded rectangles). "Talus" seemed fitting. The cute little critter on the blend label is a pika, which lives at higher altitudes, and nests within talus slopes.

The traditional method for packing a pipe with flake is not to rub out the flake then pack. Rather, one flake at a time is broken in half, then stuffed into the bowl with force. These two differing approaches provide different burn qualities, and result in somewhat different aromas. My Scree blend (see previous) is the very same blend made without pressing. They are similar in taste and aroma, but distinct.

Talus Flake
- Lemon Virginia 62.5% (10 parts per 16)
- Perique 37.5% (6 parts per 16)

Tegu: This was inspired by the Scree blend, which is a simple Virginia / Perique shred, which in turn was a rubbed version of the Talus Flake. Both of those used Virginia Bright. In a quest for a VA/Per with a fatter, rounder aroma profile, I used all Virginia Red, instead of Bright, and adjusted the proportions to compensate for the more timid acidity of the Virginia Red.

I thought a fatter, rounder lizard might be in order for this new blend. What could be better than the fat, round (and quite large—up to 4 feet long) Tegu? [The Tegu doesn't eat people or pets. It eats just plants, insects and eggs. Whew!]

With only two ingredients in this blend, the pH balance is less forgiving of variations in the particular batch of either ingredient that you use. So you may have to fiddle with the ratio, to adjust it to a tongue-neutral balance.

Tegu
- Virginia Red 75%
- Perique 25%

Photo: Michel Mazeau

The **Ténéré** is 150,000 square miles of sand, spreading from northeastern Niger to western Chad. During neolithic times, it was the center of the Tenerian culture (about 5000 to 9000 years ago), during a much wetter period. On a happy note, Ténéré contains the sunniest spot on earth. Today, wells are sometimes hundreds of miles apart.

With 40+% Oriental, and another 25% VA Bright Cavendish, this blend's nicotine is modest. Pouch aroma is somewhat floral. Smoke aroma is rich and delicious. Burn is fairly good. I get similar results with any of the Basma-type Orientals, in place of Krumovgrad. Using Samsun, Bafra, Trabzon or Katerini gives it a little more edge. Substituting India dark air-cured rather than Kentucky dark air will increase the nicotine.

Perhaps in Ténéré, someone just might walk his camel hundreds of miles for a bowl of this blend beneath a tree.

Ténéré
- Krumovgrad 40.6% (6½ parts per 16)
- Virginia Bright Cavendish 25% (4 parts per 16)
- Burley Red Tip Cavendish 25% (4 parts per 16)
- Dark Air-Cured 9.4% (1½ parts per 16)

The Barn: There is a trail shelter along the Appalachian Trail where it wavers along the Tennessee and North Carolina border, that is know as "The Barn". Not too surprisingly, The Barn is a fairly large barn. Its formal name is the Overmountain Shelter. The ground level is used by hikers for both sleeping (on the wood floor) as well as for dining. The Barn is prodigiously roomy. A ladder leads up to its spacious hay loft. The Barn offers a spectacular view down the slope of the mountain from its "veranda". Hiking northward on the AT, one can look back on it for miles, a tiny red cube in a field of green.

This blend is burley-rich, but still what I would consider a medium Latakia, English-style blend. (They even speak English in the mountains of Tennessee and North Carolina.)

The Barn
- Burley 25% (4 parts per 16)
- Latakia 37.5% (6 parts per 16)
- Virginia Red 18.75% (3 parts per 16)
- Virginia Bright 12.5% (2 parts per 16)
- Oriental 6.25% (1 part per 16)

Three Cavs: Sorry about the Edgar Hunt painting. I couldn't resist the pun. This all Cavendish blend is similar in strength to Greenbriar Two Tone (half Lemon Cav, half Burley Red Cav), but offers less of the distinctive burley taste and aroma. Nicotine is medium. A bowl of Three Cavs seems to mingle well with a bowl of any Virginia / Perique blend smoked before or after it. Three Cavs is not as "heavy" or rich as a Perique-containing blend.

Of course, the possibilities for blending Cavendish made from different varieties of tobacco are endless. In addition, Cavendish can be lightly cooked or heavily cooked—each extreme differing in aroma and blend possibilities. If a variety is flue-cured or sun-cured already, then I will make Cavendish from it as is. On the other hand, if it is an air-cured variety (e.g. burley, MD, dark-air, etc.), I always kiln it first, to finish the fermentation process.

When I cook Cavendish to as dark a color as possible, it loses much of its distinctive aroma, and simply becomes a reflection of the source tobacco's nicotine content. So don't think "Black Cavendish". That is an artifact of commercially cooked, cheap tobacco that has been rendered perpetually dark by being kept perpetually moist— the result of propylene glycol. There is no need to cook away the subtleties of a variety. The minimum cooking for any of the three varieties of Cavendish I used in this particular batch was 6 hours (thoroughly wet, inside a Mason jar) in a boiling water bath. They each retain their distinctive varietal character, though that is quite softer than the uncooked versions.

Notice my intentionally wide shred. I can manually shred (with my Kuhn-Rikon 6" kulu blade) to about half that thickness, but prefer the friendlier packing and slow burn of this wider shred.

My approach has been to find a general pH balance among the ingredients. Straight Virginia Cavendish though tasty, has a definite tongue bite. The same is true of Cavendish made from an Oriental. Most of the other varieties of Cavendish that I've made are too strong in their nicotine for me to enjoy them straight. Blending them works magic.

Three Cavs
- Lemon Virginia Cavendish 50%
- Burley Red Tip Cavendish 25%
- Maryland 609 Cavendish 25%

Three Zebras: Well...three zebra butts, at least. You can't *exactly* make this, unless you happened to grow TrabZon as the basis for making your home-fired Latakia. But you can make a similar blend with whatever Oriental variety you chose, so long as you have some of it just sun-cured, and also make Cavendish with some of it. I'm not sure how it would turn out with components made from non-Oriental varieties. Purchased Latakia works too.

As a background, all of my TrabZon was sun-cured. Some of the sun-cured leaf was home-fired with my magical brew of smoke ingredients. Some of the sun-cured leaf was cooked into Cavendish. And the remainder of the sun-cured leaf was kilned for 2 months. All of the components were shredded to a similar size, blended, then rested for a week, before lighting up any of the blend.

I find the blend soft, enjoyable. It doesn't shout, "food!", or "Kentucky!" And it leaves a Latakia room note. I could best describe this as an incense sweetness, with a cedary, clove-like tingle on my tongue.

Three Zebras
- TrabZon Latakia 25%
- TrabZon Sun-cured (kilned) 25%
- TrabZon Sun-cured Cavendish 50%

Three Zebras

Top Frog: An English-style Oriental blend

Top Frog
- Virginia Bright 50.0%
- Perique 30.0%
- Stacked Basma 20.0%

Typhoon: This blend offers a very full pouch aroma, a rich flavor, and a nicotine level somewhere between Cat 3 and Cat 4. Room note not available, since the roof was blown off.

Typhoon
- Black Mammoth Cavendish 43.75%
- Virginia Bright Cavendish 43.75%
- Stacked Basma 12.50%

Typhoon-ish
- Dark Air-Cured Cavendish 43.75%
- Any Flue-cured Cavendish 43.75%
- Oriental 12.50%

Whale Foot: If you think some people are forgetful, then consider the poor whales. They once had legs, but totally forgot about them a long time ago. ("Sweetheart, have we forgotten anything?") This blend is a study on what pipe tobacco might taste like if we envision it as a whale gently walking on its tiptoes.

Nicotine is full. Room note is subtle, like a whale foot, though I don't really sense "cigar" here. The mouth *feel* is similar to that of cigar tobacco. Aroma is spectacular. My only disappointment is that the burn is sluggish. So smoke this dry.

Long Red, specifically used in this blend, is in the same general flavor/aroma category as Pennsylvania Red, Dutch Ohio and Little Dutch. But when made into Cavendish, those all resemble Cavendish of any one of the Broadleaf/Seedleaf varieties.

Whale Foot
- Long Red Cavendish 12.5% (2 parts per 16)
- Olor Cavendish 12.5% (2 parts per 16)
- Little Yellow Cavendish 12.5% (2 parts per 16)
- Basma 62.5% (10 parts per 16)

Whale Toes
- Broadleaf or Seedleaf Cavendish 12.5% (2 parts per 16)
- Cigar Leaf Cavendish 12.5% (2 parts per 16)
- Dark Air-Cured Cavendish 12.5% (2 parts per 16)
- Oriental 62.5% (10 parts per 16)

Photo: Greek Culture Ministry

Wine Dark Sea: This ancient head of Hermes, recently discovered beneath Athens, was probably carved centuries after Homer wrote the Iliad and the Odyssey, yet the sculpture dates to 500-600 BC. The Red Wine Yeast perique, created by Steven Farmer (FTT forum member GreenDragon), is the unique ingredient of this blend. My blend uses red wine yeast perique made from Virginia red tips. It is not as alkaline as Louisiana perique, so substituting it will likely require adjusting the perique proportion downward. The nicotine strength will, as usual, depend on the tobacco variety from which the perique is made.

For the Orientals, any Basma type (Prilep, Xanthi, Basma, Izmir, etc.) can be used for the Basma component, and any petiolate Oriental (Samsun, Bafra, Trabzon, Katerini, etc.) for the Trabzon component. Or you can just create a 50:50 blend, using a single Oriental plus the red wine yeast perique.

The pouch aroma offers a subtle, red wine aroma, though this is undetectable in the smoke aroma.

Wine Dark Sea
- Red Wine Yeast Perique 50% (8 parts per 16)
- Basma 25% (4 parts per 16)
- Trabzon 25% (4 parts per 16)

Wine Dark Sea

Winter Ptarmigan: A merging of FTT forum group think.

Winter Ptarmigan
- Oriental 22%
- Flue-Cured 35%
- Dark Air-Cured 7%
- Cavendish 36%

Yellow Frog: It is Basma rich, pH balanced with Perique, and offers a modest dose of Latakia. A gentle sort of frog. If you enjoy a smooth, mild, lightly floral pipe tobacco with a nicotine in the range of mild-but-definitely-there, this a blend to put on your list.

Yellow Frog
Basma 68.5% (11 parts per 16)
Latakia 15.75% (2½ parts per 16)
Perique 15.75% (2½ parts per 16)

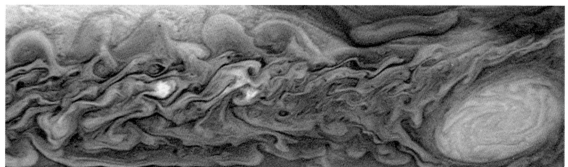

Zeus: This is a rich English/American style Balkan. The WLT Double Bright Virginia contributes a light though distinctive flue-cured taste, without the edgier acidity of VA Bright. The combination of Burley Red tips and Maryland Cavendish cranks up the nicotine to medium-full, and rounds-out the flavor profile. Despite one quarter of the blend being Latakia, its smoky-incense taste and aroma seem to remain in the background.

Zeus
• Virginia Double Bright 37.5%
• Burley Red Tip 25%
• Maryland Cavendish 12.5%
• Latakia 25%

The author.

Celebratory Appendix

Bob's 74th: It was February of 2022. I saw this secret message as a challenge. I had purchased a huge, "Party Size" bag of potato chips. The "best if used by" date was my upcoming birthday! Was it an omen? At the very least, I would clearly need to settle a new pipe blend ahead of that date. That is what would be best.

This is a mild to medium strength blend. I have enjoyed it at any time of day. Flavor and aroma present a broad, though soft profile. Pouch aroma is likewise subtle, though the small quantity of Perique can be discerned. Have a Happy Bob's 74th Blend Party!

Bob's 74th
- Maryland 50%
- Flue-cured Virginia 31.25%
- Oriental 6.25%
- Perique 12.5%

Made in United States
Orlando, FL
23 November 2022

24895721R00049